GOLDEN HANDCUFFS REVIEW

Golden Handcuffs Review Publications

Editor

Lou Rowan

Contributing Editors

Andrea Augé
Hélène Aji
Louis Grego

In memoriam Louis Rowan

LAYOUT MANAGEMENT: Louis GREGO & Presses de la Rue d'Ulm

Libraries: this is Volume I, #35

Information about donations and advertising at:
www.goldenhandcuffsreview.com

Or write to: Editor, Golden Handcuffs Review Publications
c/o Righi, 14036 23rd Pl NE, Seattle WA 98125, USA

All work belongs to authors and artists. Spring, Summer 2025.

Contents

THE WORK

Jerome Rothenberg

Hélène Aji
    Jerome Rothenberg Programmatic 11

Rae Armantrout
    Jerome Rothenberg: A Tribute 29

John Olson
    Making Any Everything: A Tribute to Jerome Rothenberg
    (December 11, 1931 - April 21, 2024) 31

Hank Lazer
    Shortly after Jerry passed away... 37

Essays

Hélène Aji
    "Improbable Imprints": David Antin's *Definitions* (1967) 39

Simon Smith
    Humming the line *to The Magic Lantern Slides*: kaleidoscopic
reflections on Maurice Scully's *Humming*. 57

Fiction

Philip Terry
S is for snake 69

Ken Edwards
DECAY, for large mixed ensemble. A score for
performance 76

Brian Marley
Extract from Crime, My Destiny 84

Meredith Quartermain
Odyssey 93

Peter Quartermain
Un-doings. 97

Interviews

The Quartermains
Personal Geographies: Meredith interviews Peter
during lockdown 103

Jacob Siefring
[In the Port of Possibility] Interview with Joseph McElroy 114

Poetry

Tony Baker
Two poems 140

Joseph Donahue
REVEALED, REVEILED. A suite for Randy Hayes 142

Nathaniel Mackey
Sound, Sound and Summary – "mu" three hundred

fifty-first pars—.. 152

Eléna Rivera
    Three Poems 162

Aidan Semmens
    Four Poems 168

Simon Smith
    Poems 174

Harriet Tarlo
    Four Cut Flowers 182

RESPONSE

Ian Brinton
    'spirit in the bark' 184
    The Last Unravellings of the Logoclast 190

Stacey Levine
    You Know There's Something by John Olson 194

Brian Marley
    Mice 1961. 196

John Olson
    A Reflection *On Reflection*, by Brian Marley 204
    Sustaining Air: Jennifer Bartlett's biography of the life of Larry
    Eigner 207

Simon Smith
    Life During Wartime: Peter Quartermain's *Growing Dumb* 211

TRIBUTE

Françoise Palleau-Papin
  A tribute to Lou Rowan's *Golden Handcuffs*
  Review (2002-2025) 216

NOTES ON CONTRIBUTORS 222

Jerome Rothenberg Programmatic

Hélène Aji

Jerome Rothenberg is one of the very few American poets. He has moved from self-engaged inner poetry to a social poetry in a classic development, until the translation of any culture in American hemispherical geography can take its place within his broad praxis. (Mottram 163)

These are the opening words of Eric Mottram's contribution to Barry Alpert's *Vort* issue dedicated to David Antin and Jerome Rothenberg in 1975. The piece entitled "Where the Real Song Begins" is a wild dash across Rothenberg's work to date starting with the translation anthology *New Young German Poets* (1959) and ending with *Esther K. Comes to America Poland 1931* (1974). The reading method is astonishing as it proceeds through a reorganization and reactualization of quotations from both the poems and the essays by Rothenberg. The density of citation leads to a fusion of voices and enacts the processes of cultural transfer at work in the poet's poems using them as sources for a new form of critical apprehension. Indirectly what gets redefined is the very notion of an American poet, "anti-imperialistic", "democratic," "transnational" and "transtemporal" (164). With extreme conceptual clarity, Mottram transitions from the inner and outer explorations that lead to the "vision emerging in the poem." Playing with the diversity of Rothenberg's inspirations and influences, Mottram delineates a poetics that, we now know, informs many a development in American poetry as "a passage & an act of desperation" (Mottram quoting Rothenberg in *Floating World* no. 4, in 1961). For Rothenberg, in Mottram's view, the stakes are high and the balance is fragile between deep exploratory images and the demands of "transmittability" (167). The eclectic sourcing for the poems and the demand for active erudition on the side of the reader dissolve the poet's integrity into what Michael Palmer calls a "non-entity":

> As Keats knew in looking toward Shakespeare and Milton, the poet in his or her non-entity is also always double or shadow of another and another. The Whitman of democratic aspiration and open-form poetics recalls the psalmic rhythms of Blake and his commitment to spiritual revolution. Rothenberg's Tristan Tzara/Sami Rosenstock is at once the Dada poet/performer of the Cabaret Voltaire, chanting the cultural bankruptcy of a world bent on self-annihilation, and the ecstatic singer, the singer outside himself, of the Jewish mystical tradition. He is also without option the Jew in history, witness to diaspora and systematic mass-murder. When Rothenberg echoes and alters Tzara's voice (or assumes the mystic Hugo Ball's cape and conical hat), he becomes in his turn, this multiple presence, just as song becomes both Kaddish and dance, mourning and affirmation, the dark and light of an unrepresentable reality. Here too, deeper in shadow, appears the shaman, singing in what Robert Duncan interpreted as a literal *psych-osis*, a state of psyche or soul where one is double to one's self. (iv)

Constructing the poet into the site of a present reconfiguration of memory is perhaps what synthesizes these few lines and provides a starting point to any reconsideration of Jerome Rothenberg's work. Beyond the idea of "a usable past" updated to inform the present and help navigate its complexities, the process entails a radical transformation of the poet as he turns from an individuated poetic voice into the medium through which a plurality of voices can make themselves heard. As mystical transmitter, the poet lends himself to what he calls "othering" both in the sense of becoming other and of making other in a performative and transformative way. So, my project today is to move through the different dimensions of Jerome Rothenberg's work as they come to embody configurations of memory relevant to the present, and effective poetic operations designed to respond to the present's challenges. With reservations of course, this dynamic is in keeping with some of Ezra Pound's initial impulse. In Jerome Rothenberg's words:

> Pound's paganism, in that sense, was a prettier, clearly more literary proposition, closer to Eliot's classicism, I suppose, though the drift of his politics was more extreme & dangerous, getting himself bogged down in the Renaissance and so on, then with Fascism and the perpetuation of the nation-state. But think of what he contributes even so: the collage composition of the *Cantos*, the pivotal breakthroughs in translation, the sense of history as vortex, the transmission of an actual alternative tradition. (« From A Dialogue on Oral Poetry with William Spanos » *Pre-Faces* 27)

These four components of poetic action that Rothenberg outlines in the Pound heritage help organize his own activity: the anthologies are tradition-making; the translations allow for the implementation of what he calls "total translation"; the sense of history as vortex evolve into a collapse of the past onto the present and the invention of procedures to reconstruct it; the politics of poetics are revisited to converge with what Creeley calls Mottram's "sociality". It is from this political angle that I would like to revisit a few of Jerome Rothenberg's works as they keep responding to our individual and collective quandaries.

Anti-imperialistic

What is most special about Jerome Rothenberg's anthologies is that they are active—one might be tempted to say activist—anthologies. They gather under the generic term of "poems" a wide variety of documents that are systematically shown as interrelated. Their characteristics are shown as spanning thousands of years and roaming a global terrain, reinventing themselves under new conditions in a continuous, rather than discontinuous and divisive manner. In *Technicians of the Sacred* (1968), *Shaking the Pumpkin* (1972), or *America a Prophecy* (1973), the exhibits are reconsidered as much more than detached artefacts from an irretrievable past since they combine as practical variations leading to present-day poetic practices. The series entitles "The Pictures" (*Technicians of the Sacred* 26-28) thus transitions from cave paintings to cosmogonic designs and ideogrammic complexes that tie in with early 20th-century calligrams or later concrete poems. Every document is the opportunity to propose a possible lineage as well as the occasion to question any notion of qualitative progress. The modes may change but they do so in response to the conditions of their production rather than according to some delusion of linear improvement. From the Easter Islands to the proposals of William Blake (1825), Hugo Ball (1916), Guillaume Apollinaire (1918), Charles Olson (1953), Augusto de Campos (1964), Seiichi Niikuni (1965), or Nina Yankowitz (1978), what is delineated is a common creative repository equally shared rather than mined through predatory processes of appropriation. With *Revolution of the Word, A Gathering of American Avant-Garde Poetry, 1914-1945*, the issue is consequently to acknowledge the path to present experimentation and through this recognition to open the way forward to more comprehensive explorations:

> [To] give a sense of how we found our way to new views of our own immediate pre-history, & what aspects of those views this anthology is trying to present. For we are all, in different ways & from our individual perspectives, talking about a virtual revolution in consciousness, & if we can't remember how we got here, we may be talked into denying where we want to go. (*Revolution of the Word* xii)

This "revolution in consciousness" sends directly back to a statement by Mina Loy quoted on the cover of the volume, which brings together the inward movement of introspection and the outward movement of awareness. One of the functions of the anthologies is to clarify the poet's position in time and space rather than to compose the solid foundation for some alternative canon. To this extent, they are provisional records of potentiality in the way that makes Rothenberg refer to Gertrude Stein's convoluted formulation in *Narration* to point at the writer's condition:

> The exciting thing about all this is that as it is new it is old and as it is old it is new, but now really we have come to be in our way which is an entirely different way. (« On Anthologies » *Pre-Faces* 139)

The anthologies open onto a revision of one's understanding of intertextuality in terms of hybridization in such a way that they resonate with Edward Said's 1994 definition of the "new encyclopedic form" of modernism whose necessity derives from the disruption of ideological universals (Said 1994, 189). However, the investment, according to him, does not imply the development of alternative orthodoxies, but rather "a particular sort of nomadic, migratory, and anti-narrative energy" (Said 1994, 279): "this movement resists the already charted and controlled narrative lanes, and skirts the systems of theory, doctrine, and orthodoxy" (Said 2002, 281). The anthologies counter the will to power of imperialistic methods of citation by being seed compositions, consistently recognized as other and susceptible to reorganization and expansion in unpredictable ways.

Transnational

The migratory dimension stressed by Said is a major component of the impulse to translate and reflect on alternative methods of translation that underpins Rothenberg's practice of translation as transmission and transfer. In the preface to *Shaking the Pumpkin* (*Pre-Faces* 97), he emphasizes the emergence of the translated text as a new poem in the target language rather than an attempt at strictly conveying its meaning. This meaning remains putative, intrinsically linked as it is to the translator's personal perception of the original text. The interference and intervention of the translator as co-creator at least are not seen as unavoidable downsides: they are part and parcel of a whole theory of translation whereby the resulting poem works as a response to the source poem, inscribes itself within the context of present poetics and exposes itself to the test of its relevance to the preoccupations of that new context.

> I don't want to set English words to Indian music, but to respond poem-for-poem in the attempt to work out a « total » translation—not only of the words but of all sounds connected with the poem, including finally the music itself. (« Total Translation: An Experiment in the Presentation of American Indian Poetry » *Pre-Faces* 78)

As one might infer, the process is in part indebted to Ezra Pound's practice of translation as it focused on the overall effect of the original text, and its interpretation in the time and place of translation. The insistence on the "music" of the poem implies further constraints than the demands of lexicon and syntax as the translation moves beyond replication into the more uncertain grounds of recontextualization and reactualization. The gift of the poem maybe is what translation centers upon and aims to activate, thus defining Rothenberg's idea of "total translation":

> One way or another translation makes a poem in this place that's analogous in whole or in part to a poem in that place. The more the translator can perceive of the original—not only the language but, more basically perhaps, the living situation from which it comes &, very much so, the living voice of the singer—the more of it he should be able to deliver. In the same process he will be presenting something—i.e., making something present, or making something as a present—for his own time & place. (« Total Translation : An Experiment in the Presentation of American Indian Poetry » *Pre-Faces* 92)

The notion of "presentation" is then more complex than it seems at first, since it does not limit itself to the introduction of lesser-known texts to a wider readership. Supplemented by the reference to analogy, and the inscription of the poem in the live conditions of its production, the idea of presentation turns into a polysemic reference that includes "presentification" and a gift in the Derridean sense of the term, liberated from the economy of gift and counter-gift that cancels it and restored to its mystical experience of presence. The translation performs this renewal of presence for a text that might otherwise get lost in the flow of time and motion of displacement.

There are many examples of this ethics of translation as Rothenberg implements it with a wide range of texts. One of them is *The Lorca Variations* that are first introduced as alternative modes of reading. The postface to the volume reminds the reader that the poems also work as a form of homage and as a recognition of indebtedness. Yet, they are radicalizing Rothenberg's translation theory by dealing with the original texts as "vocabulary", a repository of words from which one will draw the words of new poems. This extension of the translation act into procedural composition is what makes the translation total, in the sense of complete:

I felt a frustration in not being able to publish my own translations independently, thus diluting whatever sense I had of doing a Lorca homage, etc. With that in mind, I began to compose a series of poems of my own ("variations") that draw on vocabulary, especially nouns & adjectives, from my translations of the Suites (later from *Poet in New York* as well) but rearrange them in a variety of ways. [...] these poems both are & aren't mine, both are & aren't Lorca. The methods used resemble chance operations but with a margin of flexibility, with total freedom in the case of verbs & adverbs, with occasional addresses to Lorca himself embedded in them. The result isn't translation or imitation in any narrow sense, but yet another way of making poetry—& for me at least, a way of coming full circle into a discovery that began with Lorca and for which he has stood with certain others as a guide and constant fellow-traveler. (« A Postface » *The Lorca Variations* 90)

Performing more conventional translations of the poems turns out to be but one step on a longer journey to transfer the Spanish poems into world poems. The return of the text as "itself and not itself" signals the double-bind of presentification: it simultaneously revives the past text and seals its loss, as in the last poem of the volume, « Coda : The Final Lorca Variation ».

the end for Lorca comes
only when we let it   helpless
with insomnia we hear him stir   we see him
reach for Saturn
rising overhead

no homage can repay what we have lost (87)

This might help us better account for the difficulties of, for instance, the seventh Lorca variation, "Water" dedicated to Charles Bernstein (16-17). One is tempted to elucidate the dedication and trace the explicit references to Bernstein's poetry, that would get reformatted into the language of Lorca. But this might obliterate the way the poem works as an enactment of Bernstein's theory about absorption and the unperceived ideological discourse inscribed in the very structures of linguistic expression. Despite the Lorcan impulse to free the poem from the strictures of conventionality and recover the energy of elegy through lexical sobriety and the simplicity of images, Rothenberg's text remains poised on the verge of mystical crystallization and the reader is prevented from achieving any kind of epiphanic discovery. "Black" rather than "dark", the text precludes the transparency that could have allowed for transcendence and confines its reader to the materiality of words and images. The "lake" comes with its baggage of pathetic fallacy and meditative *topoi*, but the mention will not coalesce into intertextual reference because it is not sustained. The iteration of these cognitive disruptions generates the "beehive" effect of a disturbing buzz that imprisons the poetic subject into a "crystal prison". From the idea of transnational transfer that translation implied, the poet extends the corrosive power of his activity to dissolve more than the boundaries of nation or self, maybe achieving Gayatri Spivak's "unrestricted economy of same and other" where no text stands ancillary to another (*Postcolonial Reason* 424).

Transtemporal

A corollary of this dissolution is a type of haunting of the text that ends up materializing the haunting of the poet himself, and more generally, the condition of haunting that is a shared human condition. This haunting has no specific theme but, with Rothenberg, it is tragically mediated through the internalization of the Holocaust, and a succession of attempts to render the claustrophobia of impossible mourning. One might believe, as Eric Mottram suggests it, that the poems of *Poland/1931* aim at investigating the poet's personal version of primitiveness, and making it mesh with the collective version that is the make-up of America. From Polish shtetl to New York, hinging around the year of the poet's own birth, a series of poems constructs a narrative whose main feature is their phantasmatic dimension. In his conclusions about this 1974 collection (the latest at the time of his writing), Eric Mottram points out the collage pictures that insert the poet's image among the crowd of shtetl men, women and children as it paradoxically foregrounds both the presence and absence of this lost world. With analogous effects, the exploratory piece "Jews &" that can be found in the Rothenberg archive at UCSD summons a list of relations that could be a mode of redefinition of a fluid identity: it does not exist in and per itself but is modelled along its interactions with otherness. The list is presented in reverse alphabetical order, from the Z of "zinc" to the A of "arabs" somehow retracing the steps of a catastrophic migration from the metal roofs of Polish houses to the conflict and violence of Israel's creation (MSS 10 Box 28 Folder 17).

```
         JEWS &

                              page one

         jews & zinc
         jews & wounds
         jews & willows
         jews & weeping
         jews & veins
         Jews & twitches
         jews & that
         jews & tetanus
         jews & teeth
         jews & silence
         jews & shame
```

page two

jews & sailboats
jews & razors
jews & prowess
jews & poison
jews & nothing
jews & moans
jews & melting
jews & mammon
jews & ladders
jews & joy
jews & joined

page three

jews & glass
jews & flames
jews & fish
jews & famine
jews & deathless
jews & deeds
jews & crosses
jews & conscience
jews & bulk
jews & baggage
jews, arabs

END OF SET ONE

The poem reads as some endless litany of unresolved, and potentially insoluble, conjunctions. The words are spelled out, brought forth to consciousness by their materiality and the constant reminder of their inscription in a vocabulary of pain that might be as numerous as the dictionary.

This haunting of language can (and does in Jerome Rothenberg's work) move into several directions. With *Khurbn*, the book of disaster, the poet experiences one extreme instance of "othering" as mythologized in the figure of the dybbuk. The silenced voices of Holocaust victims roaming the apparently placid Polish countryside of the 1980s find their channel through the poet's body, turning him into the medium for their expression.

> The absence of the living seemed to create a vacuum in which the dead–the dibbiks who had died before their time–were free to speak. It wasn't the first time that I thought of poetry as the language of the dead but never so powerfully as now. [...] There was a reason for [not wanting *Poland/1931* to be a poem about the Holocaust], as there is now for allowing my uncle's khurbn to speak through me. The poems that I first began to hear at Treblinka are the clearest message I have ever gotten about why I write poetry. (*Khurbn* 3-4)

Khurbn is a gesture of testimony to the impossibility of total erasure, the desire for revenge and rebirth, and the permission given by the living to the dead to inhabit them.

> at night their voices
> carrying across the fields
> to rot your kasha your barley
> stricken beneath their acid rains
> no holocaust because no sacrifice
> no sacrifice to give the lie
> of meaning   & no meaning   after auschwitz
> there is only poetry   no hope
> no other language left to heal
> no language   & no faces
> because no faces left   no names
> no sudden recognitions on the street
> only the dead still swarming   only khurbn
>   (*Khurbn* 14)

Written "after Auschwitz", it is a response to Adorno's imperative, its subversion as it begins to envision the new "barbarian" language that is the post-Holocaust language of the poem. It develops into a literalization of this possession with the gematria poems. Temporality is cancelled as all layers of historical experience are shown to cohabit within the very matter of language.

In *Gematrias Complete*, published in 2009, Jerome Rothenberg indeed presents as a coherent whole poems composed over more than fifteen years, and published in installments since 1994. All of the poems expand from a method initially devised to compose the poems of *14 Stations*, a series based on the 14 names of 14 Nazi death camps, and their transcriptions into Yiddish. All of them are written according to a complex compositional strategy that starts from the Hebraic transcription or translation of a word, often a name or a noun, that is then processed as a seed word for further combinations and compositions. The use of the Hebrew alphabet for transcription, and of Yiddish, rather than Hebrew, as the target language opens the door to a mystical world of Kabbalah whereby alternative modes of textual interpretation can be developed using the numerical value of Hebrew letters and the total value of words as additions of their letters' value. Words of identical value can then be hunted through the text of Torah, which works as a vocabulary or word repository. These words can be used to compose poems built on the links thus created, so that words are related to one another that would otherwise have remained unrelated. The numerical logics creates a web of signification that is counter-intuitive, divorced from the free association of lexical fields or poetic inspiration. In the specific case of the Nazi death camps, selecting the words of equal value to the name of the camp allows to build a vocabulary of "related" words of equal value in the Hebrew of the Biblical text, which once translated into English make up poems that speak to the original name but do not directly express individual affect or the subject's perception of the disaster of Holocaust.

This process of linguistic circulation imprints on the poems the seal of estrangement, defamiliarization, and alienation in language as well as in the apocalyptic landscape of post-Holocaust poetics. Yet, when moving on from the names of death camps to the names of fellow-artists and poets, or to common nouns, the poet expands the purview of his initial intuition from a recognizable historical disaster to the conditions of ordinary living: the complex modes of expression, and linguistic manipulations convey the difficult day-to-day survival of a consciousness. The potentially infinite poetic series unfolds texts that constantly remind their reader of the loss of the source text, and metonymically of the loss of original experience, through the practices of iterated derivation and interpretation.

As an import from Hebrew, and a practice of reading and interpreting texts in non-linear, paradigmatic rather than syntagmatic fashion, gematria upsets conventional modes of approaching texts, as well as provides hypotheses for post-deconstructive reconstructions. According to Jerome Rothenberg it is a "poetry of numbers"[1] based on the numerical value of words, and the relations that can be traced between words of equal numerical value as they appear in the text of Jewish Torah. The networks of signification thus outlined can be deemed subliminal, not so much in the sense of being perceived unconsciously but, quite on the contrary, in the sense of being imperceptible but through intense deliberate investigation and calculation.

> While numerical gematria and coded temura come easily in a language like Hebrew which is written without vowels, the possibility of similar workings in English shouldn't be discounted. Gematria-generated poems can also be composed by translation from Hebrew [...]. The fact of translation may, in fact, add to the apparent "distance & power" of the combinations, a direct relationship that twentieth-century poets like Reverdy saw as the basis of the poetic image. (« Gematria » *Pre-Faces* 159)

> For myself the numbers have been a presence beneath speech, but I have known them also, being Jewish, in the letters of the alphabet I work with. My father drew them with his finger on the kitchen table. And I have lain awake like him & counted numbers in sequences that play on mind & body until the rhythm of numbers, letters, shapes, & forms is inescapable—as still another source of naming. (« The Poetry of Numbers » *Pre-Faces* 157)

More than any other strategy maybe, gematria combines the mechanical techniques of depersonalization, that cancel personal choice and

---

[1] Cf. « The Poetry of ds mbers » *Pre-Faces* 156.

inspiration, with highly idiosyncratic formal decisions, that generate tense poems reflecting a verbal haunting. In this context, the Torah provides for a vocabulary to restore the un-narrativized, and possibly un-narrativizable complexity of human experience, while gematria-generated poems produce a potentially infinite array of alternative discourses to approximate it.

On a level, Rothenberg's gematrias are memorial poems, that send the reader back to a tradition, intrinsically linked to a collective Jewish textual world, to the patriarchal word, and to his personal initiation into the poetic. On another level though, the poems witness the remanence of a disappeared object, subject, or event that has lingered in the very letter of each and every word. The tension is thus figuratively inscribed in language itself between the autonomy of the single word, and its relational intensity, as each word is objectively linked to an unexpected, and largely unsuspected lexical network. This lexical network generates other paradigms and, as Rothenberg puts it, an alternative way of "naming" or defining. A single word can radiate and resonate into several possible relational constructs that are springboards for interpretive variations and alternatives.

THE VOICE (1)	THE VOICE (2)
will answer	A voice.

(*Gematria* 43)

In the two "voice"-based gematrias, voice is simultaneously defined as existing only as part of a dialogical communication system, as a singular instance, and not as a generic abstract notion. Doubly the mathematical links between the words (or within the word itself as a matter of fact) posit definitory statements, that can be seen as complementary (1), and divergent (2).

So, it is significant that the first experimentation with gematria as a compositional mode should have happened with "14 Stations" (*Seedings* 99-116). The poems occur as part of another series of poetic attempts to provide some modicum of poetic witnessing for the missing witnesses so eloquently evoked by Girogio Agamben in *Remnants of Auschwitz*. Agamben reflects with Primo Levi on the witness by proxy that is the defective witness of the Holocaust: beyond the horror, one must confront the paradox of witnesses whose reliability is compromised by the very fact that they remain as witnesses. The "value of testimony lies essentially in what it lacks" (34) says Agamben. The total witness cannot rise from the dead to bear witness; the testimony of the defective witness is threatened because it is mediate. It is threatened but not cancelled however, since it falls into the category of speech acts. According to Agamben following Foucault in *The Archaeology of Knowledge* (1969), the testimony is valid as a verbal event, an enunciation that can be studied as a positioning of the subject, beyond the linguistic modes of text analysis, by focusing on the "taking place" of discourse (145). With Jerome Rothenberg's gematrias, the mathematics of language generate the discourse for the impossible witnessing, by imprinting the horror in the words themselves, and as a consequence, in all words, so that poems change in their very nature as they deny consolation, and remain forever bogged in disaster. The process goes as far as to contaminate the sacred word repository that does not contain them, since the names of the death camps are not in Torah: they are out of bounds in that sense, but the text does circulate their numerical equivalents. The words of the prayer, to extrapolate, are literally reinvested by death itself which they indirectly state rather than compensate.

With "14 Stations," history is collapsed into a textual projection that imprints the unspeakable past onto all of language, all its uses and all its users. Once it has happened it may remain enclosed and be lost in the memory of the deceased, but it will also vividly resurface as it has stayed imprinted onto every word of a shared language through a system of linguistic equivalence. The distressing side effect of this procedure is that the names of the camps do stay out of reach of the analytic voices, as well as of the poetic voices, but still make themselves heard everywhere: the event, the words for it, and the images, in the shared visual work combining the poems with Arie Galles's arial drawings of the extermination camps, are erased and activated at the same time, a figuration of the aporetic witnessing that presents and subtracts the event in one and the same gesture (Galles 26).

Through the use of the gematria-related modes of composition, Jerome Rothenberg brings in historicized components, as well as an organization that might temporarily narrativize them, but he also generates conditions of testimony not unlike those articulated by Giorgio Agamben in *Remnants of Auschwitz*:

> We give the name *testimony* to the system of relations between the inside and the outside of *langue*, between the sayable and the unsayable in every language—that is between a potentiality of speech and its existence, between a possibility and an impossibility of speech. To think a potentiality in act *as potentiality*, to think enunciation on the plane of *langue* is to inscribe a caesura in possibility, a caesura that divides into a possibility and an impossibility, into a potentiality and an impotentiality; and it is to situate a subject in this very caesura. (Agamben 145)

Democratic

Thus, the open-ended processes of Rothenberg's "othering" outline the paradigmatic potentialities that characterize a reconfigured rapport to language. They speak against authority for a consideration of the human in its many guises and disguises. In that sense, they are powerfully reminiscent of Hannah Arendt's warning against totalitarianism and its propensity to "invent a system in which all men are equally superfluous"

(433). What Rothenberg's poetic gestures are consistently attempting is, in Arendt's words, "to create—not merely discover—a new foundation for community as such" (436). One is then impressed by the clairvoyance of Eric Mottram's reading of Jerome Rothenberg's early poetry, and his use of concepts that have come to full visibility and relevance in the more recent poems of *The President of Desolation & Other Poems*: the texts stand witness to an enduring commitment to the poetic as "inclusive" (168), "connective" (171), and "intersectional" (179), and as the means to postpone disaster yet a little longer. But the poems also remind us of the precariousness of this temporary *equilibrium*, since we are all sleeping in a room of mirrors, that is also Hitler's room "at the Hotel Monopol in Breslau":

> In the room
> Where Hitler slept
> Dreams didn't come
> But sounds
> Broke from the walls

(*The President of Desolation* 98)

WORKS CITED

Agamben, Giorgio. *Remnants of Auschwitz: The Witness and the Archive.* Daniel Heller-Roazen, trad. New York: Zone Books, 2002.
Arendt, Hannah. *The Origins of Totalitarianism.* New York: Harcourt, Brace, and Co., 1951.
Galles, Arie Alexander. *Fourteen Stations/Hey Yud Dalet.* Morristown, NJ: The Morris Museum, 2002.
Mottram, Eric. "Where the Real Song Begins." *Vort* no. 7 (1975) 163–179.
Rothenberg, Jerome. *Gematria.* Los Angeles : Sun & Moon, 1994.
Rothenberg, Jerome. *Khurbn.* New York : New Directions, 1989.

The Jerome Rothenberg Papers. MSS 10. New Poetry Archive, Mandeville Special Collections, University of California San Diego.
Rothenberg, Jerome. *Poland/1931.* New York : New Directions, 1974.
Rothenberg, Jerome. *Pre-Faces and Other Writings.* New York : New Directions, 1981.
Rothenberg, Jerome. *Revolution of the Word: A Gathering of American Avant-Garde Poetry, 1914-1945.* Boston: Exact Change, 1974
Rothenberg, Jerome. *Seedings and Other Poems.* New York : New Directions, 1996.
Rothenberg, Jerome. *The Lorca Variations.* New York: New Directions, 1993.
Rothenberg, Jerome. *The President of Desolation & Other Poems.* Boston: Balck Widow Press, 2019.
Said, Edward W. *Culture and Imperialism.* New York: Vintage. 1994.
Spivak, Gayatri Chakravorty. *A Critique of Postcolonial Reason: Toward a History of the Vanishing Present.* Cambridge: Harvard University Press, 1999.

Jerome Rothenberg: A Tribute

Rae Armantrout

Everyone who knows poetry, knows Jerome Rothenberg's groundbreaking anthologies. I was only about twenty-two when I somehow got hold of the first one, *Technicians of the Sacred,* first published in 1968. That book presented translations of mainly Indigenous poetry and song from around the world, placing, for instance, creation narratives from the Maoris of New Zealand and from various Native American peoples alongside a translation of the book of *Genesis* from the Torah. To say this was eye-opening is an understatement. In the late 60's, many of us were looking for a way to *re*-enchant the world. *Technicians* was a guidebook for that project.

At this moment of growing nationalism and xenophobia, Jerry (he was Jerry to me) is an exemplar of openness, eagerly inviting the other in. His most recent (and now posthumous) anthology, *The Serpent and the Fire,* edited with Javier Taboada, presents poetry of the Americas from pre-Columbian times to the present day. His desire to bring together what has been kept separate (and unequal) was unflagging even as his health failed.

His own poetry, coming as it did, in the immediate wake of the Beat generation, has sometimes been not gotten enough attention, especially in America. (He was often, however, invited to give readings elsewhere in the world.) His influences were global and ranged from indigenous poetry, to European surrealism, Dada, Yiddish songs and Hebrew chants. In his poems, he often speaks as an outsider for whom the place in which he finds himself is strange. He is part exile, part explorer. I use the word "exile," because the multi-generational trauma of the Holocaust haunts his work. In one of his books, *Kurbn*, a Yiddish word meaning total destruction, he visits the town in Poland fifteen miles from Treblinka) that his family came from and evokes the absence of the lost by describing an empty "honey street", its shops and stalls standing eerily deserted. It's also true, however, that his poems are filled with a stubbornly ecstatic celebration of the sensual and the visionary. His repeated references to Blake's "burning babe" bring together these seemingly opposed trends. In these lines from his poem for the start of this century, "Come into this World," he is both exile and stunned time traveller—not nostalgic, but amazed to have survived and to find himself *witness* to a new millennium—shocked into simple visionary clarity.

> Like a clock my heart
> moves closer
> to the burning babe
> & stays there.
> I will now count
> the century
> by ones & twos.
> This morning
> all the voices in my dream
> spoke with one voice.
> *I feel privileged to be here*
> *among you.*
> From now on
> we will live
> on borrowed time.

His poems feel urgently apt now, as the world slides toward fascism again.
I feel privileged to have known Jerry Rothenberg. I very much wish he was still here "among us." He, along with his wife Diane, was a wonderful friend and host. As in Jerry's anthologies, their table brought together artists, thinkers, and writers from around the world. He created new spaces and invited us in. I will always be grateful.

Making Any Everything: A Tribute to Jerome Rothenberg (December 11, 1931 – April 21, 2024)

John Olson

I never had the pleasure of meeting Jerome Rothenberg, but his presence over the years had an almost uncanny palpability to it, which stemmed from the immense impact two of his anthologies had on me, *Technicians of the Sacred* and *Revolution of the Word*. These anthologies powerfully affected the way I thought about poetry, and were as pivotal to my evolution as a poet and writer as the invention of writing itself, or the first time I travelled down the Meuse river on Rimbaud's drunken boat.

    I discovered *Technicians of the Sacred* while browsing in a bookstore in the early 70s. The title excited my attention: I loved the oxymoronic pairing of those two concepts, the divine and the pragmatic, and everything they implied: the divine was real and there were tools available to access its power. Tools that were as vital to the art of poetry as a non-contact voltage tester to an electrician or a Geiger counter to a radiologic technologist. These were instruments sensitive to invisible energies in the same manner certain twists and distortions of language were capable of accessing other dimensions and reenchanting the world. The concept of a profession, such as a priest or rabbi or Imam, whose mission was accessing the sacred was appealing, but more so was the more paganistic idea of poets and griots who used the powers inherent in language to achieve their ecstasies and visions.

The concept of the sacred being an element in poetry was not new to me; Rimbaud had used the word *voyant,* which translates as 'seer' in English. "The Poet makes himself a *seer* by a long, gigantic and rational *derangement* of *all the senses.*" I was keenly aware of this aspect of writing, but had neglected to explore it more fully until my discovery of Rothenberg's anthology. *Technicians of the Sacred* would serve as a crucial, invaluable manual in the proceeding years. And the name Jerome Rothenberg would alert my attention every time I saw it in print, particularly if it was in relation to Dada, which was another of Rothenberg's interests, which at first seemed like an entirely different world, but the more I gave it thought seemed bizarrely relatable in the context of ancient spells and invocations. There was a commonality there that spoke to something far larger than literary convention. Something uncanny as snow.

The first poem I turned to was an Eskimo prose poem titled "When Houses Were Alive":

> One night a house suddenly rose up from the ground and went floating through the air. It was dark, & it is said that a swishing, rushing noise was heard as it flew through the air. The house had not yet reached the end of its road when the people inside begged it to stop. So the house stopped.
>
> They had no blubber when they stopped. So they took soft, freshly drifted snow & put it in their lamps, & it burned.
>
> They had come down at a village. A man came to their house & said: Look, they are burning snow in their lamps. Snow can burn. But the moment these words were uttered, the lamp went out.
>
> (Told by Inugpasugjuk)

The poem filled me with euphoria. I knew exactly what it was talking about, and it provided a marvelous solution: remove your head. Don't let your thinking, your tendency toward the analytical and expository ruin the trance-like beatitude generated by an immersion in language and the hypnopompic facility with which words flow, unblocked and uninhibited by the rational, but most especially by the vanities of authorship and the need for ultimate control.

There's a ton of material in this book, but the way it is organized is a big help. The book is divided into 11 sections, organizing the work by category and geography: Origins & Namings, Visions & Spells, Death & Defeat, The Book of Events (1), The Book of Events (II), Africa, America, Asia, Europe & the Ancient Near East, and Oceania. There is also a generous quantity of commentary in the back section, excellent insights and speculation culled from what is known about the chiefly oral cultures from which most of the work has been gleaned.

For example, in "Three Teton Sioux Songs," Rothenberg cites his source – Teton Sioux Music by Frances Densmore – and gives a fascinating explanation of how "The lines in Densmore's translation correspond to single words in the Sioux; thus each word of Sioux equals one line of English. The result, accidental or otherwise, is to isolate the poem's structural properties (of stops & starts, disjunctions, etc.) as basis for a new music of utterance in the translation, providing a notation (including the parenthetical additions) that closely parallels – remarkably so for the third songs – the sound of much contemporary poetry in English," and presents Robert Creeley's "I Know A Man" as a contemporary echoing of Sioux prosody. What I mostly love about the work in this book is the perpetual surge of immediacy, the exhilarating artlessness of the visions and spells and origins and namings presented in this volume. Read it long enough and with such increasing absorption you begin smelling burning wood and red ocher and kangaroo grease. The staleness that sometimes creeps into the pretentiously literary is absent. In its place are events, such as burying the skull of a yak or old men building "a stone fire and the men inhale the smoke and squat over the fire in order to allow the smoke to enter their anuses." (Do not try this at home).

I love the bluntness and simplicity of the lines in all the work, such as the brusque and candid statements in "The Chapter Of Changing Into Ptah": "I eat bread. / I drink ale. / I hoist up my garments. / I cackle the Smen goose. / I land on that place hard by the Sepulchre for the festival of the Great God." It reminds me of Dylan's "I eat when I'm hungry, drink when I'm dry" from "Standing in the Doorway."

Rothenberg's anthology *The Revolution of the Word* fell into my hands at a perfect time. I was going through a big infatuation with Marcel Duchamp, including dwelling on his text for the *The Bride Stripped Bare By Her Bachelors, Even*, in which such phrases as "headlight child," "subsidized symmetry," "oscillating density" and "Bachelor Machine" delighted me. I thought I'd covered all the ground until – on page 28 of *Revolution of the Word* - I discovered a postcard experiment Duchamp titled "Rendez-Vous Du Dimanche 6 Fevrier 1916," in which he'd typed wildly disjunctive and imaginative prose poems on four postcards addressed to Mr. & Mrs. Walter C. Arensberg. Each are typed neatly within the bounds of the postcard with no space between sentences or shifts in thought, so that the poems resemble blocks of "apparently meaningless" text, and gives them a curious solidity. The texts are written in the neutral tone of a manual or set of instructions, and are confident in their affirmations, none of which are remotely aligned with reality. This discovery gave a happy, galvanizing jolt to my nervous system. It was exactly the kind of writing I'd been reaching for.

Revolution of the Word was published by the Seabury Press in 1974. There's an epigraph on the cover by Mina Loy: Today is the crisis in consciousness. Man, did that hit home. And now more than ever, considering the number of zombies walking down city streets transfixed on small computer screens and gaslighting and censorship and propaganda running rampant through the media. I saw a man moments ago wearing a hat that said "Make Orwell Fiction Again."

The subtitle of *Revolution of the Word* reads "A new gathering of American Avant Garde Poetry 1914-1945." So, not at all current, but still quite pertinent. Rothenberg sheds light on the intent of this work in his opening autobiography:

> It was 1948 & by year's end I was seventeen. I had been coming into poetry for two years. My head was filled with Stein & Cummings, later with Williams, Pound, the French Surrealists, the Dada poets who made "pure sound" three decades earlier. Blues. American Indian things from

Densmore. Cathay. Bible, Shakespeare, Whitman. Jewish liturgies. Dali & Lorca were ferocious possibilities. Joyce was incredible to any of our first sightings of his work. The thing was to get off on it, to hear one's mind, learn one's own voice. But the message clear & simple was to move. To change. To create one's self & this one's poetry. A process.

And concludes by saying:

For we are all, in different ways & from our individual perspectives, talking about a virtual revolution in consciousness, & if we can't remember how we got here, we may be talked into denying where we want to go.

Revolt doesn't have to be shrill, or pleading or stentorian. It can be. Doesn't need to be. Revolt isn't always political. The work in *Revolution of the Word* is transformative, "a rush of experience into the vortex," to quote Pound. The vortex being a confluence of energy, "a radiant node or cluster...from which, and into which, ideas are constantly rushing." Energy creates pattern, in other words. The voltage of revolt being "a dance of the intelligence among words."

A less likely name, Walter Conrad Arensberg, an avid art collector and close friend to Marcel Duchamp, would provide a model for the kind of writing I wanted to do, an abstract, non-syntactical writing similar to that of Clark Coolidge and Ron Silliman. This is no small statement; I can't underestimate the importance of this book, or *Technicians of the Sacred*, and the impact Jerome Rothenberg has had on my development, introducing me to sources of which I was ignorant, and coupling them to the real. The savagely real. The absurdly real.

Rothenberg's anthologies (I also own the two huge volumes *Poems For The Millenium* Volumes One and Two, which I also assigned to an extension class some years ago in a course on experimental poetry at the University of Washington). I'm a bit of a fan when it comes to anthologies. I love to see collections bound together in hefty volumes where the connections and interrelations among various entities grow like rhizomes in a stand of bamboo. I'm a sucker for amalgams, compounds, blends and combinations. Hybrids. Miscellanies. Variegations. Transitions in a feverous intensity. To quote Walter Lowenfels from "Apollinaire An Elegy," "Building is a vista or a vision / a spirit that inhabits stone or air / the persistent soul of objects / making any everything / a womb of possibilities."

Shortly after Jerry passed away…

Hank Lazer

Shortly after Jerry passed away:

Thinking of, remembering, missing Jerry Rothenberg. Times together reading and hanging out together in Paris, Rouen, London. A recent poem of mine in memoriam:

once there was
the lamp
in the spine
hidden in your body
invisible mind
emitting its burbling
thoughts thinking
like the bubbles
in a comic strip
one among
ten thousand things
he is gone now who
asked "what is life
if it
goes on without us"
it
& its visceral
insistence
5.3.2024 / Duncan Farm
<quoted lines from his book *Seedings*>

Jerry was, for me, an inspiration, guide, and ever-encouraging friend. I can't help but think of Jerry apart from his being in conversation – with Diane (at their home in Escondido – a home as shrine for the books & artifacts of his perpetual travels), with David Antin. Jerry's anthologies changed and opened up my sense of what poetry is, was, and could be, most especially *America a Prophecy, A Book of the Book, A Big Jewish Book*, and *The Book, a Spiritual Instrument.* Each anthology a conversation and collaboration with various co-makers of each collection. I had the honor and joy of bringing Jerry to Tuscaloosa for a reading and visit – most memorable his chanting of his total translations of the Navajo Horse Songs. His energy, passion, vision, smile, beaming beautiful eyes – indeed, "visceral insistence" that resonates, ripples outward and onward, indeed, what thou lovest well remains…

Improbable Imprints: David Antin's *Definitions* (1967)

Hélène Aji

Published in 1967 by Caterpillar Press, *Definitions* (fig. 1) is one of David Antin's very first books of poems. It gathers three series of poems that systematically question cognitive conditions and the subject's relationship to language: in "definitions for mendy," "trip through a landscape," and "the black plague/ parts I-IV," Antin is preoccupied with the capabilities of poetic expression to converge with the complexities of actual experience. What are the ways of accounting for a series of events, individual and collective, that threaten sanity, the integrity of the rational mind, and the relevance of its logics? How to make the disruptions legible, and the cognitive breakdown tangible?

The design of the book is part of the strategies to respond to these quandaries: it is specific in that it foreshadows the irreconcilable inner contradictions that shape (or misshape) the poems. It was created by Eleanor Antin, the poet's spouse and a performance artist whose work articulates the undermining of master narratives, formal expectations, and uses irony and discrepant stagings to foreground the artificialities and absurdities of human social configurations.

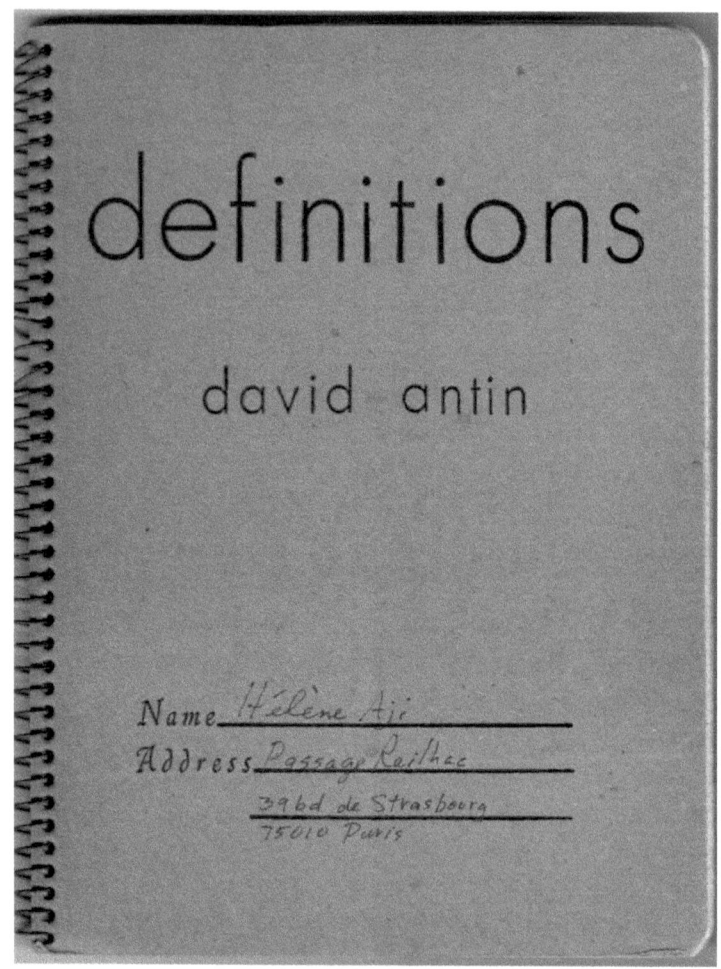

(fig. 1)

An index to Eleanor Antin's potential input when it comes to David Antin's poetic innovative decisions can be found in the description of their cooperative work on "Three Musics for Two Voices" in 1968. Antin writes:
> I had an old experimental design book left over from my college days and decided to use it as the basis for a controlled improvisation that I asked my wife Elly to help me with. Elly, though a conceptual artist, was an experienced actress and good at improvising. I typed out the text that I wanted her to read and that I was going to question, and

set it up so she could either respond to my questions or continue reading. We turned on a tape recorder and tried it. (*talking* 189) Along with encouraging the propension to improvise, and the use of the tape recorder as a decisive prop for creation, Eleanor Antin might also have been key in theorizing David Antin's poetic practice. In Marjorie Perloff's introduction to the collection *TALKING* for the Dalkey Archive, it is "Elly" who recognizes the poetic in the type of talk produced by David Antin, and triggers the advent of what would be his distinctive poetic form, and his major poetic statement: "When the Antins played the tape of 'Talking at Pomona' on the drive home from Pomona, Elly, as David tells it, declared without a moment's hesitation, 'that's a poem.'" (*talking* vii).

The design of this small volume thus questions the very fabrication of the poem and the book of poetry, as well as the construction of the poetic *persona*. It is an early evidence of David Antin's dislike for capitalizations, and most typographical conventions, especially when they imply categorizing, discriminating, aggrandizing, or diminishing, overemphasizing and generally preempting the reader's judgment. With *definitions*, the poems are printed in a font that imitates typewriting, with seemingly handwritten *addenda* or corrections in the hand of poet; the book is a spiral notebook but the printing does not follow the grid of the graph paper (and one cannot envision how one could type on a spiral notebook to begin with); the poems integrate drawings and splice philosophical texts, the dictionary, and other unidentified sources to produce their own disruptive discourse. More generally, *definitions* challenges expectations and normativity. The poems deliver textual material that is threatened on at least two levels: practically it might as well never have been produced at all since one cannot feed a spiral notebook into a typewriter; conceptually its improbable materiality points at the unacceptable arbitrariness of the events it actualizes. The brown copybook happens against logic, as do the events in the poems. It is a crucial piece to understand David Antin's poetics not just because it is gorgeous and a rare document but because it documents the primary issues that determined his poetic evolution and revolution. It resembles many of notebooks in the Antin Archive at the Getty Research Institute, with the major difference that it is a published conceptual work of the late 1960s, and as such is an integral part of the experiments whereby at the time a poet could try to begin to rebuild poetry from among the rubbles of Auschwitz and Hiroshima.

The present notes investigate the ways in which this particular book of poems is a "post-book," apocalyptic in its threefold approximations of disasters and post-apocalyptic insofar as it attempts to sustain the poetic in adverse conditions. *definitions* has three parts which are to be read in succession following the ternary structure of increasingly global human disintegration that informs the book.

Impossible illnesses : "definitions for mendy"

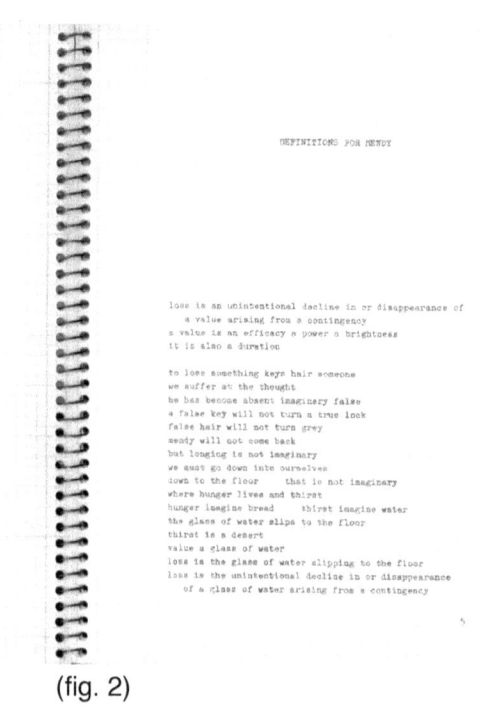

(fig. 2)

In "definitions for mendy," Mendy, the poet's friend, is dying from cancer. The poem begins on the sole constant of existence not subject to contingency, i. e. the "duration" of loss (fig. 2). The text is based on the transitivity of the verb "to be," and on the paradox of its use to describe transitionality and ephemerality. Definitions are immediately shown as problematic statements: what do we really understand from the concatenation of abstract notions that makes up the first lines of the poem? How can the poet mourn the impending death of his friend if his only tools are derealized conundrums that jeopardize understanding rather than allow it? "Loss" itself, despite the clarity of its pain-inducing general meaning, emerges as a noun that resists definition. Faced with the failure of elucidation and the deluge of vain abstract notions, the poet engages in a more pragmatic attempt to characterize loss through allegorical indirection: in moving on to instances of loss ("to lose something keys hair someone"–fig. 2), he might get closer to putting words on the actual meaning of loss. The series of lost things, "something," "keys," "hair," "someone," seems to encrypt the deeply personal and referential ("keys," "hair") within generic vagueness ("something" or "someone"), while it conveys the nature of loss as a sensation, at times precise, but at other times diffuse and objectless. The line that immediately follows, "we suffer at the thought," summarizes the affect that comes with loss, subjectivizes the experience, and adumbrates a definition that grounds itself in the losing rather than the lost. Consequently, the obstinacy of the poet in defining concrete instances of loss is defeated in the same way as the abstract attempts: by the bottom of the first page, the materiality of the "glass of water" loops back on the "value" of the initial definition of "loss," cancelling whatever delusion of progress and improved clarity the reader might have caressed. Contingency affects not just the concepts whereby the subject tries to make sense of the world but the very objects that inhabit this world, to the extent that no stable signified can be found among the constantly shifting, intransitional, opaque signifiers. What seems to be left is the perception of loss, as a pervasive state rather than a transitory experience.

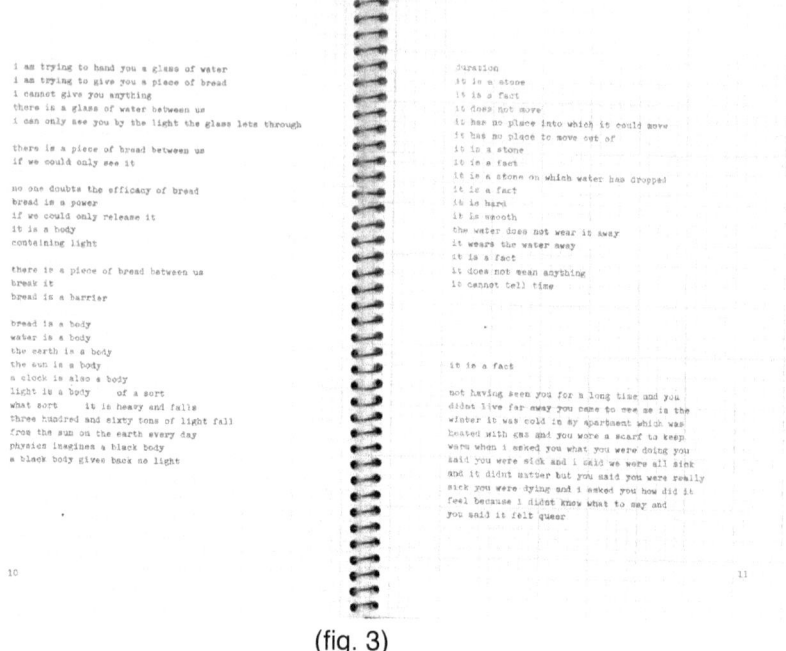

(fig. 3)

To fail to see through "the glass" of water (fig. 3) is thus not a mere Romantic reminiscence from Coleridge, surfacing amidst the tragedy of personal loss, or an invitation to revisit the elegy. It ties and contrasts the scientific approach of the dictionary with the wild inventions of the imagination. To break through the barriers that hinder perception is a repeated attempt that stumbles against the materiality of the real. By defining bread and water, the earth and the sun as bodies, what gets defined is *the* body, beyond the primary meaning of *our* bodies. Our body occasionally loses keys and hair, but above all chronically suffers at the thought. If everything is a body, including light, the massiveness of mass collapses into the « black body that gives back no light ». The black hole of astronomers is the point of highest materiality at the same time as the point where the methods of induction from concrete experience to abstract generality fail.

What to do then of the persistence of the poem in attempting these transfers from the familiarity of things ("stone," "water," fig. 3) and the routines of perception ("hard," "smooth") to the constants of definition? If thwarted conditions of cognition can make us take as fact that the stone "wears the water away," how can we recognize the actual fact of erosion? Similarly unable to recognize the fact of dying in the dying friend, and experiencing it as one's own death to the friend, the poet literalizes the flippancy of a commonplace cliché of consolation: "we are all sick" (except that we are not…) and all dying (except that not in the same conditions and temporality, not with the same intensity and immediacy). Generalization shunts realization, and the recognition of "the fact" so that the actuality of conversation brings about a cognitive shift. With the question "i asked you how did it / feel," (fig. 3), the enjambment postpones, thus highlights, the irruption of affect that definitely unhinges factuality and the semblance of objective narrative. The transcribed answer "you said it felt queer" is here to be understood as pointing at the defamiliarizing, decentering and othering that simultaneously separates the two subjects in conversation as they try to communicate. Access to the other's reality is irredeemably barred, and this obstacle, although real in any interhuman relationship, is in the instance of healthy David and dying Mendy brought to paroxysmic obviousness.

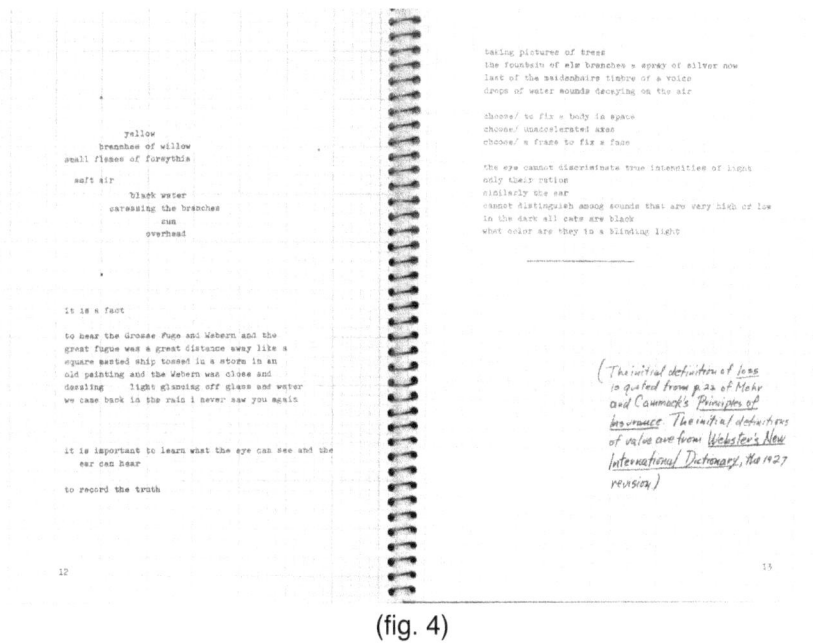

(fig. 4)

So just like the blinding light of the atomic blast, the absolute of definition is a decoy—it does not allow to see the black cat in the night (fig. 4), it does not bring the dead friend back: "I never saw you again." It is a fiction for insurance companies and dictionaries that obliterates the truth of relations and relativity. In the second part of Antin's book, this quest for normativity turns into a horrendous deadly contamination.

Unthinkable Poisons: "trip through a landscape / the car / the bird / the inside of the bell"

From Leonardo da Vinci's notes on unnerving powders used on the battlefield in the Renaissance (fig. 5) to the gases in the trenches of WWI, the Cyclon B of the extermination camps, the radiations of the H bomb, the napalm of the Vietnam War, and stockpiles of weaponized nerve gases of the Cold War, the poem moves on from the highly personal mass destruction by cancer to the collective mass destruction by human madness.

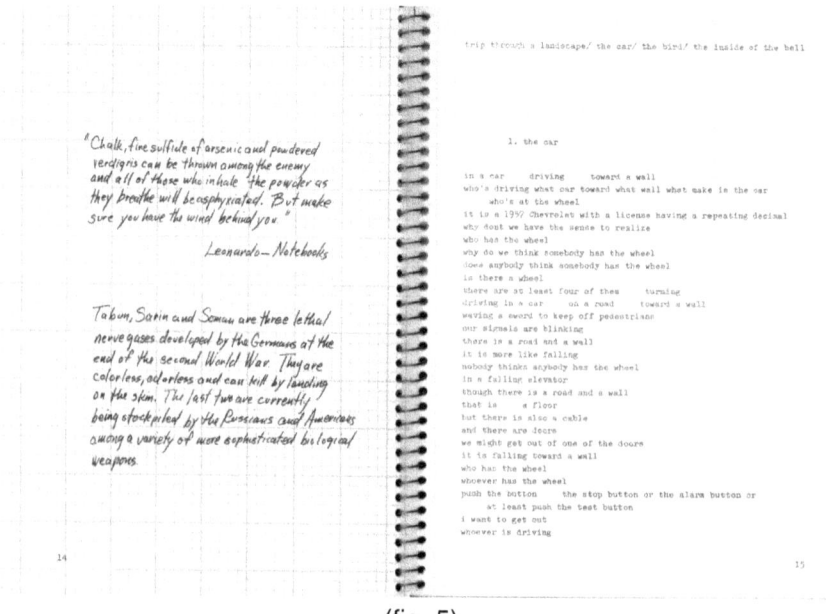

(fig. 5)

What is this landscape through which we travel? Is it a waste land in the Eliotian tradition? What is this car we are driven in? Is there no one to drive it as in William Carlos Williams's poem about America going crazy? What is this bird we might want to see in more than thirteen ways to finally get in touch with the world in Wallace Stevens's undecisive manner? Are we deaf to the bell that is tolling for us? Even after John Donne, even after Ernest Hemingway? The intertextual depth of the apparently repetitive trivial lines is staggering, raising these questions with an urgency that turns into an emergency with the sense of impending catastrophy as day-to-day accidents are summoned into the poem. The hypothetical dimension of radical apocalypses mitigates their reception so that they need translating into the matter of real near-by accidents ("a car driving toward a wall," "a falling elevator"–fig. 5) and of habitual nightmares. The images might barely touch the skin but the realities break through it like deadly poisons to bring about devastation.

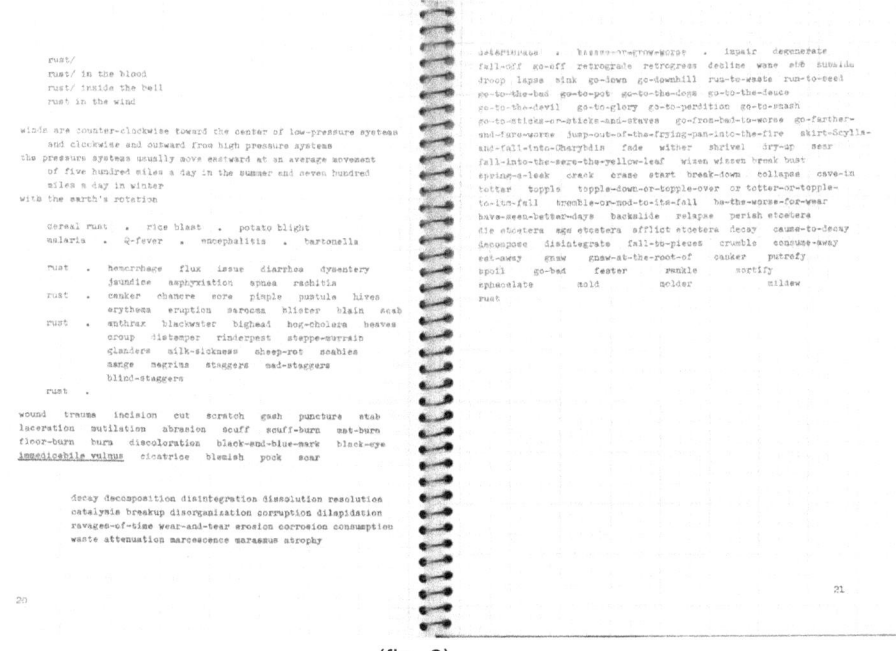

(fig. 6)

The failure to adjust expression to the realities of this destruction triggers the disruptive method of the list (fig. 6). Either copied from the thesaurus or lifted from the encyclopedia, the list foregrounds the corrosive action of definition as it shifts our attention from the panic-inducing reality of destruction to the derealized expressions of its modalities. The shortcomings of language to account for the real might thus not lie so much in the lack of words to say it but in their very proliferation: so many words for the monosyllabic « rust » engender the same defusing of meaning in the same way as the study of winds forecloses the eventuality of a hurricane. The music of dentals ("decay," "decomposition," "disintegration"–fig. 6–) echoes the eponymous "definitions," and resonates with the impending advent of death. The sounds might lull the reader into the soothing aesthetics of the poetic but they only delusively alleviate the fear that they in fact activate. The listings exhibit the way the mechanisms of language corrode the iron of reality ("rust") and euphemize the unstoppable processes of destruction. The poetic example however contaminates linguistic activity at large (in a way that prefigures the processes of the Antinian talk poem of the 1970s): the associative dynamics at work in the list, sound-based, lifted from the dictionary, or built-up from random declensions, is part and parcel of any and every exploratory cognitive process. The human mind's intent search for knowledge turns out to be the cause for its pervasive sense of "loss" (fig. 2), and "atrophy" (fig. 6), the viral point of origin of the "black plague" (fig. 7) that generally infects humanity.

Unspeakable Pandemic: "The Black Plague Parts I-IV"
The first part of "The Black Plague" starts with an autopsy – an exploration of the body made only possible through its death. The violence of the aggression that crosses through the skin and flesh to the bone is not lessened by the urge to know that is supposed to permit it. The destruction simultaneously grants access to knowledge and prevents it, irredeemably sealing in death the secret of life it seeks to discover. The shift from "auricular" to "oracular" (fig. 6) confirms the esoteric implications of the process that disturbingly diverge from the declared scientific purpose. The intention is at least equally objective and subjective, rational and mystical.

(fig. 7)

The anaphora on the word "demonstration" echoes the lists of the previous part of *definitions*, and plays on the polysemy of the term interlocking science and ideology, description and interpretation, epistemological exploration and ethical preoccupation. What is thereby demonstrated is that the scientific is ideological: the biological mechanisms of eyesight, with their constraints and limitations, entail the questioning on vision as dialectically tying perception and projection together. The mind plays on the products of vision, diffracting the initial sight through layers of distortions: "why does the eye see a think more clearly in dreams than in / the waking imagination" (fig. 8). The run-on-line plays on the reader's expectation of a comparison between dream and reality, emphasizing the ever-elusive nature of the real, never actually to be seen.

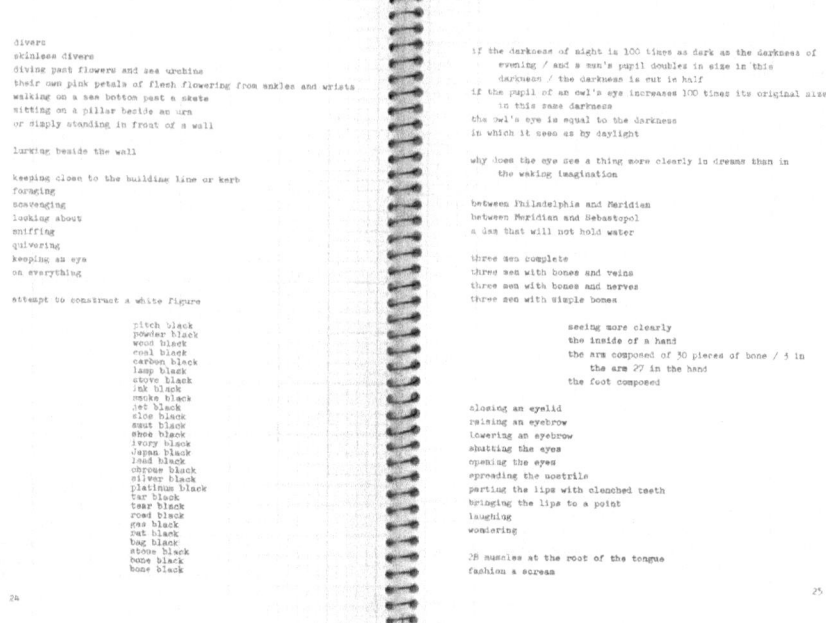

(fig. 8)

The paradox of seeing in the dark gestures towards a typology not of sight but of blindness, whose hierarchy is defining by degrees of not seeing. The biology of eyesight cannot be separated from the biology of blindness, the positive and the negative coexist in ways that might make them interchangeable: what if the certainty of vision were just a delusion triggered to compensate for the unavoidability of blindness ?

Similarly, the anatomy of the scream fails to account for its actuality: can one believe, even for an instant, that the "28 muscles at the root of the tongue" actually make the scream (fig. 8)? To the contrary, the contaminating power of analysis works to erase the immaterial existential distress that generates the scream to the benefit of its material, mechanical actualization: the scream for what it means is cancelled by the focus on the anatomy of the tongue. Conferring scientific objectivity for the sake of objectivity results in a form of desensitizing that Antin aims to counter: his lists and diagrams paradoxically reactivate the empathetic process through the "demonstration" (fig. 7) of the limits of their accountability.

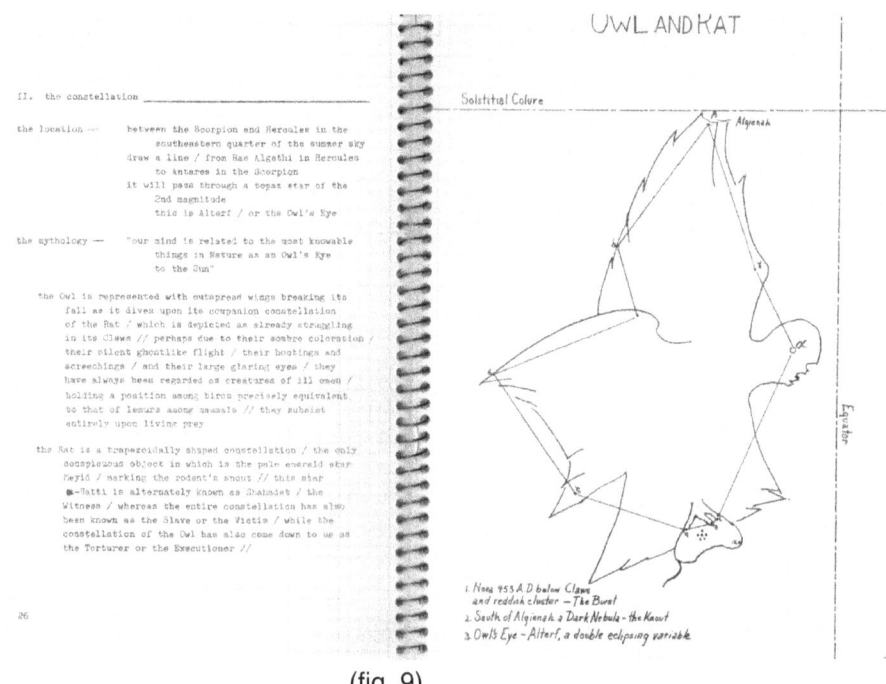

(fig. 9)

In his description of the universe, Antin consequently emphasizes how the constellations are transfigurations of a human experience of the world, transforming the unfathomable immensity of undecipherable and meaningless realities into the stage of familiar scenes. Symptomatically these scenes are scenes of predation embodying the destructiveness of the human. The only possible reading of the meaninglessness of outer space is a reenactment of a scenario of destruction. The constellation's diagram reads into the interaction between slave, victim, executioner and torturer as an omen of the endless tragedy of humanity (fig. 9). Humankind's claimed power of naming exports the violence and coercion turning every element in the world into a metaphor for its controlling and destroying impulses. From the factuality of place ("the location") to the fiction of self-projection ("the mythology"), there is no transition but dramatic contiguity. In Antin's text, these realities coexist on the same level as alternate realities of equal power—or to use the fraught term of "definitions for mendy" of equal "value" (fig. 2).

(fig. 10)

They may spell out "the grammar of pain" but do not convey "the meaning of pain" (fig. 10 and 11), since pin might turn out to be without meaning, as the rest of the random facts that are tirelessly rationalized and narrativized, so as to make contingency acceptable. As typography indicates, we are divorced from pain by the very desire to elucidate it in terms of meaning. The poem undermines its own foundations on the Adamic power of naming. Far from entailing knowledge and communication, the function of assigning words to realities cuts the subject off from reality and deadens the aggression of sensation. Implying a perception of the world based on pain, the poet hurls the reader into a psychotic cognitive condition that points toward the anesthetic effects of aesthetics.

(fig. 11)

(fig. 12)

The "image of pain" (fig. 12) is the mediated reality in which David Antin stages us, as we narrativize experience to keep it at a safe distance and maintain the unsustainable fiction of life as a story of progress and accomplishment. "Our language" (fig. 12) is thus shown as a projection which "fashions" reality in a similar manner to the way the "28 muscles of the tongue fashion a scream" (fig. 8). The informing power of language is in this respect a deforming power that reduces the radically diverse into the uniformous same, so that we can construct a community of identical beetles (fig. 12).

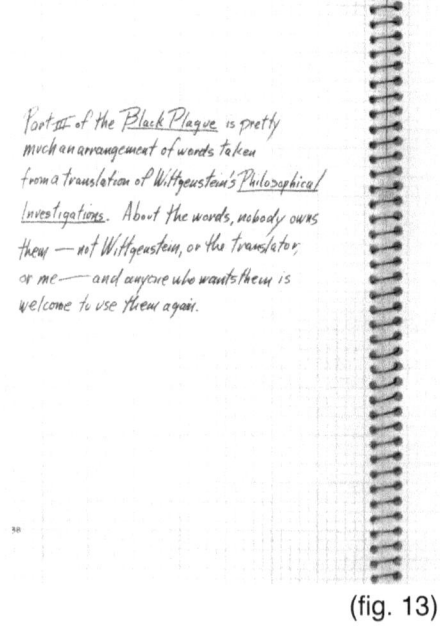

(fig. 13)

From his reading of Wittgenstein, Antin extracts the words to show the human mind bumping against the walls of language to break through to the level of Impossible, unthinkable, unspeakable realities. If anyone and everyone "is welcome to use" those words, it would none the less be a delusion to think that they "own" them, or that they can appropriate them.

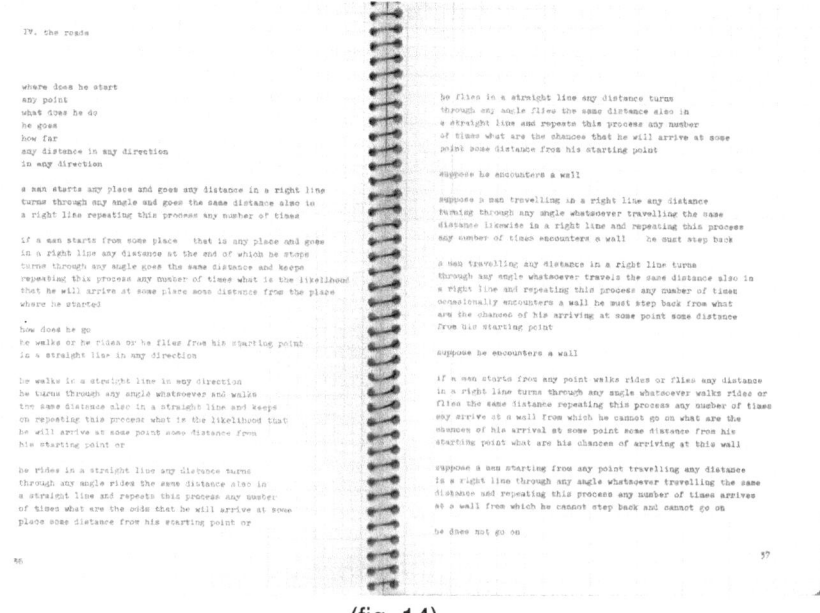

(fig. 14)

These words are "the roads" (fig. 14) to a wall from which, once it has been reached, man « does not go on ». The denial of this pragmatic realization opens the door to dreams of the infinite and the ignorance of the basic fact of the finite.

As early as 1967, then, the improbable printing of these poems stands as a testimony to David Antin's negative capability: the poet is not a prophet, and the poem is not visionary. But occasionally and provisionally it encrypts "a beetle in a black box" that is not everyone's beetle or maybe not a beetle, or nothing at all. These realities are refractory to "definitions," they come after the fall of language and the apocalypse of rationality. The improbably typewritten poem in a spiral notebook over some useless grid gestures towards the improbability of all texts and the decoy that all books are. Their claim to define the world and us is vain as duration corrodes them and death contaminates them from the smallest cancerous divergence of cellular activity all the way to the cosmic absorption of a black hole.

Antin's *Definitions* initiate a life-long interrogation over the materiality of the poetic text whereby human language-bound delusions of control are debunked, writing is imperatively happening off the grid, and perceptions shift in ways similar to the way the caterpillar of the publisher's logo morphs into an uncanny human fetus struggling for survival (fig. 15).

(fig. 15)

WORKS CITED

Antin, David. *definitions*. Caterpillar, 1967.
Antin, David. *talking* [1972]. Introduction by Marjorie Perloff. Afterword by the author. The Dalkey Archive Press, 2001.

Humming the line to *The Magic Lantern Slides*: kaleidoscopic reflections on Maurice Scully's *Humming*

Simon Smith

HUMMING THE LINE TO *THE MAGIC LANTERN SLIDES*:
KALEDOSCOPIC REFLECTIONS ON MAURICE SCULLY'S *HUMMING*

Slide 1
I first met Maurice at the 'Cambridge Conference of Contemporary Poetry (CCCP)' in 1992. We read together on the Sunday morning of the weekend conference, striking up a friendship straightaway. We didn't meet often over the years that became the decades which followed, but when we did the camaraderie was still there. Maurice was someone who I would have been friends with outside of poetry, but over the years we exchanged books and pamphlets, letters, later emails, notes. Whenever I stumbled across poems of his in magazines or online, they were some of the first I'd read, to tune into what was going on with the latest iteration of what became *Things That Happen*. I felt I was taking new bearings, resetting my own course along the way. Occasionally, he'd drop me a line on a postcard saying how much he'd enjoyed something he'd seen of mine. It was always reassuring when one of these dropped onto the mat, somehow completing the circle of composition, knowing the poem had found its way to as sophisticated a reader as Maurice. Small acts like these lead to a sense of a community, a community of poets, and we might be alone most of the time, but not so mad and alone as we might fear in the darker moments.

Slide 2
Humming is not the first or only elegy by Maurice Scully. The 'Sonata' section of *Things That Happen* 'had a circular motif to tie things up, the elegy for Ric Caddel at the centre, itself circular' (Kenneth Keating interview). Cycles, correspondences, tying things off – the function and shape of elegy in the work of Maurice Scully.

Slide 3
Frank O'Hara, 'A Step Away from Them,' W.S. Graham's elegies for artist friends, Denise Riley's, 'A Part Song,' Peter Gizzi's books from *Threshold Songs* to *Fierce Elegy* – *Humming* takes its place alongside these great poetries of loss in the late Twentieth to early Twenty-first Centuries. Revisiting *Humming* has helped me reengage and recognise the dialogues and correspondences the book has with this other work about loss.

Slide 4
There has been much written about *Humming* as 'elegy,' troubling over a definition of the genre and where the book takes its place there, or adjacent to other elegies. Scully himself has remarked, '[*Humming* is] perhaps a bit more directly personal, too. It's an elegy for my late brother. I've enlarged the frame and focus of normal elegy to go back in time sixty thousand years and forward to the present, and to focus on life and living culture as well as death and loss' (Satris interview). And, 'it is an elegy written in the form of a paean, to life, to the privilege of that adventure, in memory of my brother' (Keating interview). What makes *Humming* such a powerful and striking book is this enlarging of the frame into the form of the paean to life. 'Life goes on'. Fundamentally. But the point is *Humming* doesn't 'elevate' death; instead, it works out how death is a part of life, coincidentally highlighting how skewed death and associated processes such as aging have become removed from our corner of Western culture, silenced, erased. *Humming* restores death to the everyday, whilst not denying its shock and loss and pain. The only two poems in the book to touch on the immediate circumstances of the brother's death are not elegy in the traditional celebratory mode. The emotion that comes over instead is mainly anger, anger for the most part aimed at the speaker's self. Both poems are either summarising or rounding off sections of the book.

Slide 5
The first poem is subtitled 'Argument,' is an argument (or summary) in two senses of the word, as in the 'argument' of a long poem (here placed towards the end of the section, where it usually would form a kind of preface), and an argument the poet is having with himself (almost absurdly comical) about his 'career' or calling: 'I am 52. How old are you? I'm old enough to take a knife / to any letter from the Arts Council for instance regretting et cetera // . . . . You will have been a poet. Why? // What? At your age start again' (*Humming*, p. 35). It is as though the death of his brother causes Maurice to question his own trajectory and values.

The second poem is 'Song' and forms the introduction or preface to the final section of the book, 'Coda'. Both poems find their anchor in the Real with the image of the brother's watch: 'My brother is dead. His wristwatch laid face up beside his bed' (*Humming*, p. 35). 'Take yr wristwatch off and lay it on the bed – / good – its three hands – *haa, ha-ha & ha-ha-ha* / circling circumstance under heaven' (*Humming*, p. 93). The first line quoted here is the last line of the poem 'Ballad,' the second line I've cited here is the opening of the poem, 'Song' – the latter taking up from where the former left off. The former poem is in the stark, matter of fact third person, simply recording the events of the final moments. The latter poem, a re-imagining, is almost cinematic in framing the death in a stage direction, as though to fictionalise what has happened: as the shocking event recedes, the story needs to be told and retold, turned over again in the mind, reinvented even, to keep the memory alive and reimagined.

Slide 6
Of course, the image (and reality) of the wristwatch conjures the convergences of temporality, mortality, and perhaps even transcendence. There are other transmissions across the ether, conversations on the airwaves, correspondences, messages spelt out on the Ouija board, which appear then disappear to appear elsewhere, threading through the poems. 'Ballad' (p. 25), for instance, is a poem where the anniversaries of other deaths – Maurice's father's, his mother's, his sister's – weave together the fabric of memory and mourning to become manifest as the material reality of the poem. The

first poem of *Humming*, 'Sonnet Song' (p. 11), as well as playing on the old 'knock knock' jokes also chime with an echoey charm in the 'one knock for "no" and two knocks for "yes"' of the Ouija or séance. Jack Spicer's tinkering with the Ouija and séance can't be far from Scully's mind: for Spicer the Ouija is a metaphor, which functions as agency from the 'outside,' shaping poems, using the poet as conduit, for messages from 'beyond'.

Additionally, Scully can't have been unaware of other literary convergences in his use of the wristwatch as a metaphor for talking about issues of life and death. In immediate reach is Frank O'Hara's 'A Step Away From Them,' (*Selected Poems*, pp. 110-111) – 'I look / at bargains in wristwatches,' and W.S. Graham's 'Lines on Roger Hilton's Watch,' 'O tarnished ticking time / Piece with your bent hand' (*New Collected Poems*, pp. 235-237). Both poems form significant indices and points of contact for *Humming*, where Scully necessarily articulates his end of these transmissions: Scully's dialogues are not only with the dead in his family and the living reader, but also correspondences with poetry ancestors, and deeper still with the dead in 'deep' time at the Neanderthal burial (*Humming*, p.28).

Slide 7
The connection and relation between *Humming* and 'A Step Away From Them,' doesn't end with cut-price timepieces. Scully's book and O'Hara's poem are about bringing the everyday into connection with death, and they achieve this in a quite particular way, as displacement activity. In 'Ballad' (*Humming* p.35) and 'Song' (*Humming* p.93) similar forms of displacement take place to O'Hara's 'walk [or dance?] among the hum-colored/cabs' (*Selected Poems*, p.110). (Yes, O'Hara's New York is humming with street life, as Scully's book is humming with bees; the hive is another city). O'Hara's poem takes us dancing down the streets of a New York August day, with its labourers, advertisements, chorus girls, to be punctuated by 'Everything/suddenly honks: it is 12:40 of/a Thursday,' to move on again to food, a rich lady and her poodle and Puerto Ricans. Then the reality O'Hara is trying to avoid thinking about or feeling punches through: 'First/Bunny died, then John Latouche,/then Jackson Pollock. But is the/earth as full as life was full, of them?' (*Selected Poems*, p.111). Bang, bang with monosyllables. Scully's displacements are more absurd, comical, wry, even cartoonish (and with a nod Stateside) – but to the same effect and run out into monosyllables:

'From Scratch the dog to Doubt/the cat you stand (or hover) wondering if/you'll ever get to know the facts of life . . . // I doubt it thought the cat, me too, the dog, & rattled off/a raga to the neighbouring territories. Grab that knife!/I know the facts are rough. Goodbye' ('Ballad,' *Humming*, p.35). Both poets are talking about work, and the liberation of its routines, until stark, devastating, chaotic reality breaks into the train of thought and emotion.

Slide 8
The shift in addressee between 'Ballad' and 'Song,' from the point of view of 'I' in the former to 'my brother,' to the distancing 'you' in the latter, 'Take yr wristwatch off' and later in the stanza, 'Distorted places between/yr eye & the lens, yr eye & the surface, & yr eye/& yr mindbits & the world' (*Humming*, p.93) – run in parallel, as correspondences, with the shift of the sunny, personable "I" to the composed "one," the distancing pronoun, in 'A Step Away From Them': 'And one has eaten and one walks,' (*Selected Poems*, p.111) in more, hard monosyllables. 'One' is a pronoun hardly used in American English (and less and less so in Anglo-Irish English), used here to pull the reader up short, and carry on the walk, 'and back to work,' to conclude with, 'My heart is in my/pocket, it is Poems by Pierre Reverdy' (*Selected Poems*, p.111): Reverdy being the master poet in his use of the pronoun 'on,' for distance and a chilly, cubist, emotionless objectivity. The distancing of both poems is about maintaining emotional composure rather than any sense of 'the Cool' – the "hip" submits to self-control.

Slide 9
Not far distant from displacement activities is wounding in *Humming*. I've already touched on anger in the book, but close by anger is the wounding that causes the hurt. W.S. Graham in his great elegy for painter Peter Lanyon, 'The Thermal Stair' sketches out what is at stake: 'The poet or painter steers his life to maim // Himself somehow for the job. His job is Love / Imagined into words or paint' (*New Collected Poems*, p. 164). Peter Gizzi in his long poem of meditation on grief 'Consider the Wound,' opens with, 'no ideas but in wounds, I is that wound' (*Fierce Elegy*, p.43): here the wound speaks. In Densie Riley's 'A Part Song' (*Selected Poems*, pp. 138-146) the wounding and violence

of the sudden separation from her dead son take on nightmarish, metamorphosing presentations: projections of further loss, this time the daughter: 'My daughter lightly leaves our house. / The thought rears up: *fix in your mind this / Maybe final glimpse of her. Yes, lightning could*' (pp. 138); profound and recurring shock: 'Here I sit poleaxed, stunned by your vanishing / As you practice your charm in the underworld' (p. 141). *Humming* articulates further correspondence with these poems (and others), as wounding forms part of the anger of the elegy. In 'Ballad' (p.35) a knife figures twice in the poem, with letters from the Arts Council, and where 'the facts' of death become 'rough,' perhaps almost overwhelming. Finally, in 'Song' (p. 93) the wound of grief rises to the surface of the poem: 'I was carrying a little pain / in my head. There is every reason. Every reason'.

Slide 10
Then the pandemic came and brought the living and the dead closer together, the walls became thinner, and the ghosts, the Martians and the radios of Jack Spicer came closer, to become uncannily more relevant to poems speaking with clarity and with a louder volume across time and through space, speaking of the Dead and through the Dead. Spicer's work veering closer in zombie-like reactivation, becoming more truthful, more present in dialogues I was finding myself in, more real and urgent.

And then we lost four poets in 2022-2023. Alan Halsey, Maurice Scully, Anthony Mellors and Gavin Selerie. Four more dialogues and correspondences. Writing this piece on Maurice and the book of poetry I'm writing at the moment, *The Magic Lantern Slides*, both have become intertwined in places, fields, spaces where Spicerean correspondences are taking place, spreading web-like across time, between and through culture, transmitting song. As John Ashbery has also observed, this time in the preface to his translation of Rimbaud: 'Somewhere at the root of this, the crystalline jumble of Rimbaud's *Illuminations*, like a disordered collection of magic lantern slides, each an "intense and rapid dream," in his words, is still emitting pulses'.

Slide 11
Alternatively, in *The House That Jack Built: The Collected Lectures of Jack Spicer*, Peter Gizzi remarks on the functionality of assemblage in Spicer's 'serial books':

Spicer's poems begin to feel more "assembled". Each element is used within a poem like a color fragment brought up from depth; it represents some piece of a shattered mirror that is then assembled into a kind of cubist portraiture.
(*The House That Jack Built*, 'Afterword,' p. 212)

Earlier on in the 'Afterword,' Gizzi reveals the functioning of the 'present' of the poem in his remarks on Spicer's lectures:

Because of the disruption in the "time" and "timing" of Spicer's lines, his poems create a space that both the living and the dead share in the act of reading. What Spicer calls time mechanics is essentially a kind of quantum poetics through which different poets are patiently writing the same poem in different times and places. Hence the poem is always in the present; its time is outside time. The poem is not immortal because it endures through the ages but because it exists in all ages at once.'
(pp. 181-2)

This is how *Humming* speaks, Spicerean in its hauntings, at times 'pitching up' into song, humming.

Slide 12
Maurice Scully's 'Song,' at the end of *Humming*, so eloquently reveals the kinds of matrices, networks or underground mycelia at work, forming into hope, unconscious and unstoppable in a poem sequence of synchronicity and simultaneity, so crucial it might save your life:

A seam, a stitch, a line of tiny zeros in the fabric
through which twists *this* to *this*, fluid thread, un-
dancing thread, appearing/disappearing, holding to-
gether what had not been, tight, fast, in place,
tacked in, a little way on. Drop by drop, grain by
        grain . . .

POEM

"This piece of paper you have just been handed is . . .
Keep it. It advertises nothing, has no designs on you,

has come a long, long way, to here, in silence, in the
   rain, free. As *you* are. You *are*. Now:
      breathe . . ."

(*Humming*, pp. 93-94)

Slide 13
Concurrent, humming in the background, composing themselves, corresponding and co-responding to this essay, are these two poems, from *The Magic Lantern Slides*:

Slide 14
THE GOLDEN RECORD

Humming. Matrices, intersections, web, grid, mycelia, galaxies – an entanglement of light, the nodal spread starlit – a hearing out mapping. AI forms part of my body dysmorphia, the infrastructure haunted through echoes & waves. Drones seek out seeds. The signal pulsing onward into galactic plasma.

Draw me to the edge of the field unvoiced. Oak to beech whisper underground through fungi. I the hinge into the space of you, nebulae like mobiles turning. I for dispersal. I drop off the edge of the World & keep going, Icarus & father, glide high in silence, face to the stars, for beeswax & feathers.

Seeing is a field. What we know signifying in binary notation. Atoms radiate downward in a mass or a bow of rain like radio waves. Maurice sculling, coracle without ripple or shadow, heading out, holding on. Gone. Warm as Life was in the background the flecks snagged in light, the "off" & "ice" in office.

Light bumping along to the first invisible star – years away. To live in company disappearing, that's the thing, in breathy connectivity. Unpicked the light unravels the hot & cold between. Tapped in outer space, correspondences. Fields of sunflowers reflecting back in quantum entanglement.

Marked out like chalk on fabric, on material, temporary white line to permanent cut – a sketch, this body articulated in the World, rising to read the landscape, invisible. Outline to a life, humming the gaps, filler. Labyrinthine under hospitals. The wound recorded on vinyl & magnetic tape – a step away.

Surf, wind, thunder. Collateral. The wound in the world, a slight tear in the grey cloud to reveal a dazzling blue, sliver after the silver abstraction. Body maps, body imaging – a good idea, the light locked in rock. To form a cord, enter the bloodstream entire. Scatter to the four corners, encased in ice. Connection is Being.

Fighters, bombers, interceptors, drones – circulate, drop ordinance, high explosive, wave after wave. Words to music & the butterfly out of season. Humming to be alive, this flowery catalogue. Like getting back to the office, the dead letter office, for coffee, seeds & virus locked in ice crystals & permafrost.

Formed of light waves, the sound waves slower. & echo. Sheet, blanket or surface, the bells singing. Fighter pilots returned or downed. On the record, play by ear, the pronoun gendered, pulling four to eight g. Appear to disappear. The Golden Record glides onward, outward. In the capsule, on the record. Unconscious I'm there.

"0" & "1" – the future in touching distance – linear verses holistic. Only you & me & now from memory. The laser reading back, the mirror surface to a photodiode. One & zero, face off. Wind, wave or sun. Touched. Off on, on off, on. To blackout. The wound the record. Is to regain consciousness & listen out.

First Alan, then Maurice, Anthony, Gavin. & is the earth. Is it? Heading out. Life as full or blown as dust & pollen, them gone. Mapping wave formations – wave after wave after – murmuration after murmuration, upward, left then right, spirograph, roulette patterns, yellow flowers. Of them. & one walks. I'm gone.

Vibration or hum dispersed with the seeds parachuting through air, this quadrant of the solar system, my patch, my Being, the web in which we correspond, space opens out, in which living & dead exist, speak. Networks, webs – fibrous, even the stones sleep through the green lash, & I won't be long: answer in the echo.

Slide 15
THE GREAT FILTER

A humming. The fiction that escapes illusion: the picture its own planet, stars outside its frame. Last night the moon turned full cycle, that phase fully in the cold light, pulling the g's, the loss of peripherals. Fact, the sky crunched up, granular – inelastic demand goods, the trade in water futures. Your future.

The sound barrier. Along the perforated edge, the seagulls, shadows sideways & homeless then up, the networks, the grid words fall through: into darkness, Maurice falling, & father. The pathogen real as a paperweight. A sleight of hand. All the dinks & bumps are characteristic of exile, traceable & fact.

Ice melt accelerating at both Poles. Snap the moment, photograph the fact, History has collapsed, we love you get up! We deduced from the dangling modifier the husband was dangling. Big Bang calculations out of sync, the Universe veers off course like a gyroscope. Or a plane falling, falling.

Dear father, dear M., ride the balance of the raft, like a stick, like a blade. Wobble its makeshift half-life, between feeling & fact, an afterlife of face & fact, face unseen hooded, face unseeing shaded, half-lit, speaking as a witness speaking as a passenger speaking. Whisper then surveilled. Veiled & fact.

On quiet days I can hear the earth turning the hum. Silent. In the kitchen, off the corridor, I know you're there, rested in the jamb. Listening to the World & the World listening to me, humming the note. Fact. Limited to what we see. The note a fact, the listening you. His finger marked spectacles.

There are to be no reversals. Quantum, off the scale, real. Animal, vegetable, mineral. Fact. 35mm shutter snaps the fact. The off & on position. The World listening to you, where the photos can dissolve like soap. The old note or facts falling. Particle there, Universe there, the whine recedes. Slight.

Go on. The ghosts are calling, *sans* narrative, but with a story to tell, mouthing like fish, silent flowers gasp into the atmosphere, cloudy & clouding, rolling up the thermals. Old note to tread without sound. Trigger. Or consequence. Fact. We, halfway there, between you & me, proof of Einstein's relativity.

The starling murmuration, the black sun, circulate like nanoparticles. The bleaker the future, by probability. The Antarctic air, breath motionless then disappeared, a world unfinished. 12,000 Emperors slip off the edge of the World. Downy feathers can't hold the water away for insulation.

'Like a playing card. Red roofs against the blue sea'. What escapes first, what escapes fact. Each slide frames a moment then gone, & the accumulation of slides relates existence, a history like you were there, the dangling facts out of the air. The future linear: we are there camping out, or halfway.

There can't be too many particles & there can't be too many switches. As trade winds translate into trade routes particle & fact fall silent. The future bleak: the Empire Line to Kingston. Blackjacked. Shake & we are. A magic lantern slide, will-o'-the-wisp, known locally as the jack-o'-lantern.

Riding pillion. The hum through the things, the air, the only thing you know: how I'll miss this earth, slows the particulate reality down, blown into particles in part to switch out to switch to, flip in part switch unresolved ear up close open silence, "come on, Maurice, let's go home," humming the route.

Slide 16
RESOURCES

Gizzi, Peter. *Fierce Elegy*. (Wesleyan University Press, 2023)
Graham, W.S.. *New Collected Poems*. (Faber, 2004)
Keating, Kenneth (ed.). 'Introduction,' *A Line of Tiny Zeros in the Fabric: Essays on the Poetry of Maurice Scully*. (Shearsman Books, 2020)
O'Hara, Frank. *Selected Poems*. (Carcanet, 1991)
Riley, Denise. *Selected Poems*. (Picador Poetry, 2019)
Rimbaud, Arthur. *Illuminations*. (Carcanet, 2012)
Satris, Marthine. 'An Interview with Maurice Scully,' *Contemporary Literature*, Vol 53., No. 1 (Spring 2012)
Scully, Maurice. *Humming*. (Shearsman Books, 2009)

Scully, Maurice. *Things That Happen.* (Shearsman Books, 2020)
Spicer, Jack. *The House That Jack Built: The Collected Lectures of Jack Spicer,* (edited with an Afterword by Peter Gizzi (Wesleyan University Press, 1998)

NOTE

Whilst I was writing 'Humming the Line: Reflections on Maurice Scully,' I continued to work on my book manuscript THE MAGIC LANTERN SLIDES, a sequence of prose poems of eleven paragraphs each, started in early 2021. As the 'Reflections' developed it became clear that these ruminations were a slide show themselves, culminating with slides 14 and 15, 'THE GOLDEN RECORD' and 'THE GREAT FILTER,' both of which are included in the book and appear here, in the essay, dovetailing the two projects together; as though the memories and reflections, the grief over the loss of Maurice 'dictates,' a la Spicer, those Magic Lantern Slides into the essay.

S IS FOR SNAKE

Philip Terry

Oonce apon a toim the craic was good. It was a long toim ago now, but I know it for a fact through the tales we've been tellered, passed by word of mouther from snake to snake ofer the genererations. We'd loy in the sun on a smooth crock when it was feen, I can envisage it now, clear as dayloight, doing nobodaddy no arm, just flipping ourselfers ofer from toim to toim, or twinning ourselfers togiddyer, taking in the eat, sundereaming. It fed us, It flickered us, it made us feel all chargered up and ready to goo. Without a good sunnering from toim to toim we grew sluggish, and moody too, loik the nematodes who livered under the crocks, shunning the dayloight which brought us so much deloight. Dayloight and deloight, ther oon and the seam fer us, fer we deloight in the dayloight and the dayloight deloights in us too, so it does. When it was awet, which offen it was, to be sure, we'd swimmer in the streamers and the brooks, grubbing a flash or two for lynch, or a few shrews from beneath the bullrushes that loined the banks with their pokerfaces all soft and fluffed up loik they all is are. The shrews were plentifuller back then, and just the roight soize for a noice little sneck. If we wantered sum ting to wash dem down, dere were all is plenty of errggs to swaller, which we'd pinch from the nests of the bigcrests and gobble down whole lettering the shells crush inside us with a luvverly muffled cracking. We livered with the brocks and the bigcrests and the bears in a gree in the green land the two-legs called Irelonde, for they were full of ire, whether they came from here or from ofer the big watter, they were all is bashing each udder till oon of dem came off the worse and could bash no more. The oons who bashed no more they'd leaf where they were for the redbeaks and the nematodes, or they'd dump dem in a bog and leaf dem dere to rot though they didn't rot as we could see plain as dayloight as we swimmered by dem they just shrunk and took on a brownish colour loik the stinkin shoe leather worn by the two-legs. Offen, just to make sure, the two-legs would cut off the heads of the oons who bashed no more, or cut off their arms so that they couldn't do dem any more arm. The two-legs had some bad habits. In their stories we're the badoons, they think we're malevolent, evil craythurs, banished to the dark places and the moors, but the truth is that we're armless. Quoite literally. We make our hames where udders would foind it difficult, in crocky crevices, next to the meanderering streamers and bogs, in the shadowy glens of Irelonde, the Emerald Isle, that's anither of their noimes for it, not because it is full of emeralds, it isn't, but because it is all is green, because it is all is raining. Some two-legs think it's a bit soggy, but we loiked it loik that, so long as the sun came out now and again.

Though we gotter on feen with the two-legs, we gave dem a woid berth on the whole and they did the seam fer us. They knew we were dangerous, and we didn't want to get crushered beneath the hooves of their horses loik. Occasionally oon of dem would catcher us up with a forked stick and skin us to roast ofer a fire, but generally speaking they didn't loik to eat us, we were dark and unwholesome craythurs they mutteruttered, unfit for consumption. That's where their stories about us, all balls, came in handery. The noicest two-legs were the oons in the big capers with the beards down to their waists, fer dem we were actually holymoly, and they'd honerer us by leafing food out fer us: bigcrests, nuts, moice, berries, and a brown sticky liquid that made you shiver then a moment later made you hot all ofer. But all that changered when your man showed up in Irelonde. He came from ofer the big watter, from a londe called Englalonde, and he had the new faith on him, and carried it about in his handers in the shape of a cross. It was a large cross, made out of silfer and decorated all ofer with emeralds which glistened in the loight of the sun. This two-leg was called Pádraig, and his reputation in preachering travelled before him loik a thunderclap. It was said he was a great miracle worker: he'd cured some lepers he'd met begging by the roadsoide armed with nothing but a prayer loik, and he'd restored the soight to a bloind two-leg in the uplondes, by simply replacing his oyeballs with the oyeballs from a just-killed sow, as well as snatchering oon of the daughters of an Ulster chieftain, Macool, out of the arms of a wicked demon, an act which was richly rewarded by the chieftain, and bitterly resented by his daughter, who ran away in tears and threw herselfer into a nearby river. He travelled all ofer, sleeping in the open with only a crock for a pillow, and whenefer he came across a great hill, he would climb it on his handers and knees, no matter how diffidiffcult the way, until he reached the top where he would raise his arms to the heavens and cry out in his loudest voice, preachering about his oon and oonly nobodaddy who ruled ofer all things, the londe and the big watter and the heavens aloik, who demanded that we throw away false gods and give our allegiance to him and to him alone, amen.

We looked on from the safety of our crevices in the crock, tongs flicking, curious yet wary about this strange and charismatic two-legs and his preachering, whose influence went from strength to strength as he kept performing strange and fantastical miracles. He was said to have raised from the dead a mither who had died in childerbirth, togiddyer with the twins in her womb, and when the twins came out into the woid world they could patterpatter from the moment of their birth and preacher the word of nobodaddy in the Latin tong. And then oon day he took on his bitterest rivals, the oons in the big capers with the beards down to their waists. It was on his way to Kells that he met three of the two-legs in the big capers with the beards down to their waists, who stood in his path, blocking his way loik. They told him to goo back to Englalonde where he had come from udderrwise they would changer him into a crock and throw him down a well that had no bottom. Pádraig laughed at this which angered the oons in the capers with beards down to their waists, but when dey tried to work their magic on him dey could do nothing to him. Pádraig turned his oyes to the heavens and prayed to his nobodaddy, and his nobodaddy answered not in word but in deed, changing the oons in the capers with beards down to their waists into three frogs, who croakered in unison, then jumped off into a nearby bog, never to be seen again. Brékkek Kékkek Brékkek Kékkek! Kóax Kóax Kóax! Now he had ofercome the two-legs in the capers with their long beards, he turned his oyes to us, the craythurs that were holymoly in the oyes the bearded two-legs. We were not holymoly any more, he said, spitting his words out loik venom, those toims were ofer, we were nothing but pure evil, for it was our koind who had brought sin and division into the Garden of Eden and thence into the world corrupting our first parents by tempting Eve to eat of the fruit of the Tree of Knowledge. He'd efen been sinduced by oon of our evil koind himselfer, so he had, a woman in snake form named Brigid who had given herselfer to him on a mountain top when he was moinding his own business, fasting fer all he was worth, until she had come along to interrupt him. Once he'd had his way with her, In his fervent zeal he struck her ofer the oyes with his big cross, and vowed to rid the londe of our presence, to cleanse Irelonde of our slithering forms for oonce and for all.

We watched helplessly from the hills, fear and panic spreading thorough our rankles, as Pádraig's words turned the two-legs against us. They emerged from their hovels at daybreak, gathering in packs, and proceeded to hunter us down without mercy, torching the bracken to drive us from our hames, so that the whole londe was fillered with smoke and the smell of burning flesh hoverered in the once pure air. When we emerged from our hoiding places, dazed and bloinded by the flames and the acrid smoke, they were waiting, fury in their oyes: with their knotty clubs and their long turf cutters' spades they beat us to to a pulp in our hundreds, leafing us to rot in the open air, prey for wolves and redbeaks. Their croize of anger and triumph fillered the valleys and the bogs and the mountains, until the whole isle was soon reduced to a smoking wastelonde as far as the oye could see. Those of us who escaped the onslaught fled in bloind terror, seeking refuge in the remotest corners of the isle, but there was little chance of escaping their relentless persecution. We knew we were only buying toim, and that sooner or later they would catcher up with us, for their furious zeal showed no signs of abating.

In desperation, those of us who remained gathered togiddyer on the cliff tops, our scorchered and bloody scales trembling with fear and defoiance. It was an existential croisis, not in the philersophical sense used today by some of our local tinkers – not local to Irelonde, but local to where I'm sat writing here and now, I'll come to that all in good toim – but in the sense that our very existence was under threat. We whisperered among ourselfers, trying to understonde why we were being cast out, why our peaceful existence was suddenly under threat of extinction. There was no question, Pádraig and his holymoly nobodaddy were at the root of it all. And the two-legs constantly mutteruttered about our forked tongs, seeing these, which were nothing but an evolutionary quirk to help us sense what was going on in our immediate environment, as a sign of evil, a sign of double-talk, a sign of impurity and corruption, by means of which we had tempted the oon they called Eve to eat of the fruit of the Tree of Knowledge and abandon the true way of nobodaddy. It was a simple case of scapegoating as we used to say, othering as some of our local tinkers have it, and what they said about double-talk was a load of old claptrap, language is always double-talk, you can try all you loik to say what you mean and mean what you say, but you'll never get to the bottom of it, what you mean to say in the end will always lie ofer the next hill, loik the crock of gold at the end of the rainbow. It was all balls the lot of it, but the two-legs swallered it whole loik a crab apple. There seemed to be nothing we could do about it but sit it out, until the two-legs came to their senses. Our conference had reached a dead end, and we were settling down for the night, gathering what warmth we could by twinning ourselfers togiddyer in the gloaming, when we suddenly heard the sound of footsteps, the unmistakable sign that the two-legs had caught up with us. They had us cornerered, to be sure, for we had no way to retreat any further, asides from hurling ourselfers ofer the cliff and putting ourselfers at the mercy of the snot-green big watter and the crocks some hundreds of feet below.

We hunkered down in the grass, making ourselfers as small as we possibly could, in the vain hope they might not clock oyes on us. We heard their steady steps approaching, our hearts in our mouths. They were curiously quiet, we were tinking, they were not shouting or banging their long spades on the turf to flush us out, nor did they set fire to the bracken, which would have taken in an instant. What were they up to? Were they trying to surprise us? And then we saw their faces, not the faces of the vengeful two-legs we had been expecting, but the gentle faces of the oons in the big capes with the beards down to their waists. We come in peace, brothers, they said. Like you, we have been driven out by the two-legs and the holymoly oon. We're in the same coracle. Once we'd settled down a bit and gotter talking, they told us how they had been driven out of their hamesteads and had retreated, loik us, into the wilderness. And they told us of the loys that Pádraig had been spreading about dem and about their beliefs. Pádraig, they said, had pointed to the three leafed clover as a sure sign that nobodaddy was the oon true god. The clover, he said, was a sign of the holymoly trinity, the father, the son, and the holymoly ghost. Claptrap, said the oons in the big capes with the beards down to their waists. The three leafed clover, they said, was an ancient symbol of the isle, rooted in its history like the bracken and the bogs and the rain. It was a sign belonging to the ancient beliefs that lay rooted in the londe itself, and it told how the bigcrests of the air and the craythurs of the earth, and the flash in the streamers and the big watter were all part of oon big family living togiddyer in a gree. As we talked we drank their brown sticky liquid that made you shiver then a moment later made you hot all ofer, rememberering again the ancient tales, the stories passed down through generations, of a power efen greater than Pádraig's. A power that dwelled within the earth itselfer, a primordial force that could shield us from arm. And with a unity born of survival, we called upon this ancient magic, with the help of the oons in the big capers with the beards down to their waists, drawing upon the very essence of the londe we called hame. They told us to twinner ourselfers togiddyer and form a mass, which we did, twinning our bodies the oon ofer and under the udder and the udder ofer and under the oon until we were all knotted togiddyer loik into a slithersome carpet.

And then, in a moment that seemed to stretch across eternititty, a miracle occurred. The grounder tremembled beneath our coils, and a great rumumbling filled the air as the wind whipped in across the big watter and up and ofer the cliff. From the depths of the earth, a wave of energy surged up, enveloping us in its embrace. And then, as if by the hander of fate, we felt ourselfers lifted from the soil, our twinned bodies acting loik a great wing, and were carried up and away far away from the green londe that had rejected us. We soared through the sky, carried on the whirling currents of the air, travellering for days on end, until at last, we found ourselfers far from the shores of Irelonde, far from the shores of the Emerald Isle, translated into a distant land of sand and sky and little watter where we could live in peace far from the bog dwelling two-legs, and where we've been living ever since. The londe was called the Maghreb, and the two-legs who dwelt there were happy to share their londe with us, for their beliefs were of a different koind to those of Pádraig. They had their own nobodaddy, but he didn't seem to moind us, they had their own tinkers, great tinkers, and they had their own language too, and their own way of writing: it was nothing loik the Latin script of Pádraig, with its little crosses all ofer, but was sinuous and curling loik, pleasing to the oye, loik snakes twinned togiddyer across the pager. But efen as we settled into our new hame, while our bodies deloighted in the endless dayloight, which fell from the heavens from dawn till dusk so that we passed our days in endless sundereaming, flipping ourselfers ofer from toim to toim when the eat gotter too much, our hearts remaindered heavy with the memory ot what we had losl, and they have remaindered so all across the years and the years roight up until today. For though we had escaped Pádraig's wrath, and oonce again the craic was good, or good enough to be going on with, we could never forget the londe that had oonce been our owning, the green londe where we had livered in a gree, the green londe from which we had been banished by the handers of the two-legs and the holymoly two-leg they called Pádraig, and his no good nobodaddy, cursed be his noime.

DECAY, for large mixed ensemble
A score for performance

Ken Edwards

The envelope of any event is rarely symmetrical. A human life, for instance, encompasses an astonishing rate of growth, development and learning within an intensely compressed initial period (early childhood). Its flowering can be sustained over a number of years subsequently. But already at eighteen years or so, most growth and development is over; by the late twenties response times start to slow and brain decline begins, including loss of neurons and glia; and the remaining forty to sixty years can be viewed as an extended process of decay.

At the largest scale imaginable, that of the universe itself – best considered as an event that is still in progress – physicists have proposed that the four fundamental forces of nature separated and atomic particles formed during a series of epochs encompassing a fraction of a second (immediately after the Big Bang). Then followed (they suggest) a period of up to four hundred thousand years during which atoms (chiefly hydrogen and helium) formed. And finally, large scale structures such as quasars, stars and galaxies became possible in a subsequent period of billions of years of expansion and cooling (during which no new gravitationally bound structures can form) – an era that still persists and whose end is unknown.

The envelope of a sound consists of three components: *attack* (head), *sustain* (body) and *decay* (tail). As the sound radiates from its source its diminution can be described by an inverse square law where the level will decline by 6dB for each doubling of distance. There is potentially no endpoint to this process. (That is, it is possible at least in theory to imagine that all sounds persist forever, well beyond our capacity to hear them.)

The proposal here is to model the processes outlined above, by generating and utilising a complex of specified sounds within a defined environment.

Close attention should be paid both to the environment within which the piece is made, and to the resources required. Preparations may necessitate many months or years of planning. A large, bounded space is essential. The interior of an abandoned cathedral or a disused motor vehicle factory would be possibilities, though in view of the extreme sound levels envisaged (see below), the steel girder construction of the latter may be preferable. At any rate, there should be as much floor space as possible, and ideally also standing or sitting space at different levels. A ceiling height of up to forty metres would give the optimal resonance.

Outside the chosen venue, note that considerable space would need to be cleared to accommodate the two aircraft runways on either side of it (see below), a consideration that has clear financial and legal implications in terms of necessary purchases of real estate, planning applications and demolition of previously existing buildings. Also needing to be considered is the provision of safe access for performers and listeners (who will of necessity be coming and going throughout this very extended piece), perhaps by means of specially constructed underground tunnels and soundproofed holding pens. Attention also needs to be paid to the construction of humane environments for the animals and provision for their care.

A general word on resources, and how they should be deployed. Planning, construction and deployment of the necessary resources are of course vital to the piece, which cannot exist without them. As has been hinted before, this process will have taken many years prior to the performance, and teams of personnel experienced in many relevant fields will have had to be deployed under the direction of a competent senior manager or chief executive. This senior manager will need to have developed a close relationship of trust with the conductor, who will be responsible for overall supervision of the performance and the performers in real time.

The number of players (musicians, singers and other performers) is indeterminate, ranging from small groupings of musicians on stage to many millions worldwide, if the resources permit, or as long as they permit.

It is recommended that the conductor oversees and guides the performance from an appropriately constructed control room within the performance area with good video and audio links both to the interior and exterior of the venue and to all participants. The conductor will have full responsibility for the deployment of the resources and their timing.

The work consists of three movements, as follows:

I. *ATTACK*

The event (or piece) begins with sound that can be construed as thunder – heard from distance – of the type that used to be simulated in theatrical and musical performances by vibrating thin, flexible steel sheets, but can be produced today as high-quality sound files. If some other method can be found, then this should be done. An initial dynamic of *molto pianissimo* should create the sense of distance. That is to say, in ideal circumstances it can and should almost not be heard at all, so that for a period of time it should not be possible to determine whether the sound, and therefore the piece, has started; and if it is perceived to have started, for how long it has been in progress, and if so, for how long it will persist.

Consider a plasma, or ionised gas, caused by a spark travelling rapidly upwards into the thunderhead. The rapid movement of the molecules can be modelled in sound, and the result stretched in time. Time can be measured by what occurs. Time can obviously be stretched to breaking point, but such a point should not have been reached yet, as the resources (instruments, in the widest sense of that word, as well as human and non-human performers) are yet to be gathered and deployed appropriately in their available forms.

The time-line envisaged for this first phase, or movement, of the piece may be of the order of a few hours. But the duration may be inexact, and will be at the discretion of the conductor. By the third or fourth hour, other sounds may begin to be mixed in, typically at this point sounds primarily created from the natural world: consider products derived from animal parts here, such as bone, skin or gut, of dog, cat, domestic cattle, elephant, antelope or deer, fowl, or marine creature, as well as wood from a variety of trees and bamboos, variously in the form of stretched membranes or percussive implements and surfaces, all suitably amplified. These will of course include large ensembles of conventional stringed instruments and percussion, to be complemented by more ad hoc assemblages and machinery. Following this, the living sounds of the creatures themselves should be deployed and added to the mix, or where live recordings of creatures actually present are not feasible, recordings may be used, or (less ideally) digital sounds may be synthesised to simulate such sounds as would occur. The physical manifestations of all such creatures should encompass sounds deriving from behaviour patterns relating to threat or flight, or cries of alarm or mating calls.

The overall dynamic level should increase very gradually over those few hours from the initial *molto pianissimo* and finally via an exponential crescendo in the last few minutes to *molto fortissimo,* or as loud as necessary or possible, at its endpoint.

Most of this movement should take place in total darkness.

For the last few minutes of the movement the jet fighters which have been previously been acquired and have been waiting all this while will be revving up their engines on the twin runways that have been constructed on either side of the performance venue. A pair of Eurofighter Typhoons, or alternatively Lockheed Martin F-35 Lightnings or F-22 Raptors, would be ideal, but clearly considerations of cost and availability will be important. As the final moments of the movement approach, at a signal from the conductor, they will take off simultaneously. The sound and vision of their take-off will be relayed on large banks of video screens within the auditorium.

Immediately after take-off the two jet fighters will be deployed in aerial manoeuvres such that their vapour trails will describe the mathematical symbol for infinity, thus:

$$\infty$$

The lights on the performance space are now brought up, revealing for the first time the hundreds of human and animal performers there assembled.
Now comes the middle section (second movement).

II. *SUSTAIN*

The middle part, which in Western classical music terms could also be termed the "development" section, involves further amplified musical sounds, including those made by the products of animals as described above, as well as the natural sounds of those animals that have been assembled. At an early point, the doors (stage left) to the appropriate holding pen are opened, and the conductor will signal for a sizeable herd of ruminants to be driven through the space between the stage and the audience. Ideally, these will comprise wildebeest or similar wild creatures, but domestic cattle will be an acceptable substitute. They will exit stage right, being returned to their specially constructed pen.
In the first half-hour or so, the jet fighters, still in the air, will meanwhile contribute their own Doppler-shifted sound to the general mix, fading, increasing in volume, falling and rising in pitch, all of this to be relayed within the auditorium. Gradually, these aircraft will remove themselves from the arena of operations, fading into the distance finally.
At this stage, sounds derived from metals and alloys of all kinds – iron, copper, brass, steel, silver, gold, even rarer metals if obtainable – will have been added to the mix. These will comprise not only sounds made by conventional musical instruments (woodwinds and brass, as well as cymbals) but also as many machines and contrivances, not hitherto thought of as being musical, as can and have been assembled. All musicians and operators onstage will be guided by the conductor from this point on through the graphic score, attached here as a 500-page document (Appendix A). At various times the focus will be on different parts of the ensemble, allowing toilet and meal breaks for all the participants (it will be necessary to appoint deputy conductors from time to time, with delegated authority, for the same purpose of affording relief).

Offstage, including in selected locations outside of the venue, various sub-events will be taking place, including controlled explosions and other locally staged performances.

A day or so into this section, the choir will be brought into the arena to perform the programme of euphonies and chants, composed using random number sequences generated from samples of atmospheric noise, which is also appended here (Appendix B). Remote choirs will simultaneously be recorded live in different parts of the world singing the contrapuntal accompaniments, and these performances, relayed over the internet, will be mixed in *ad libitum* by the conductor (or his or her deputy at any one time).

Ambient sounds from many different weather systems across the world, ebbing and flowing and relayed live, are also to be incorporated, to form a background against which the multiple harmonies and contrapuntal movements of the animal and human voices, and the improvised and composed sounds made by wood, bone, skin, ceramics and metal, can be heard.

At this point it will not be possible any longer to determine the geographical location of the piece, the sound being as much outside the venue as inside; or it would be more accurate to say it will be impossible to determine "inside" or "outside", so that the piece will resemble an object such as a Klein bottle, that is to say having no boundary that can be defined. Or we might say it is finite but unbounded (as Einstein proposed to describe the universe).

The dynamic level will fluctuate as the conductor brings in certain elements and excludes others at various times, although many aspects will be determined by other factors necessarily outside of the control of the participants. It will vary from virtually inaudible at some points to *molto furioso* in unison at others. It is suggested that the dynamic throughout should be as loud as necessary but no louder.

Great care should be taken to ensure a holistic approach, so that, no matter how heterogenous the materials of the piece might be, it unfolds as a single, recognisable entity in which nevertheless detail may be distinguishable within the events as they occur, being introduced and fading rapidly or slowly, but so that there should be no abrupt distinction between one event and the next, and yet precision being maintained in so far as it is possible.

About two thirds of the way through the movement, or at a point estimated to represent the golden ratio (familiar from the structure of works of art and music of the past, but also used in the analysis of financial markets), a tempo suggesting the human heartbeat, ie sixty beats per minute (60bpm) approximately, should be introduced, this to be marked initially by sections of the percussion, at first well buried in the mix yet clearly discernible, and slowly becoming more prominent as more of the musicians are directed to join in. The tempo should vary little or not at all (with the possibility of variation – the degree of *rubato* – at the discretion of the conductor) until the conclusion of the section.

By now all resources available and all possible other resources should have been consumed; this is the point at which the movement can be brought to an end.

The entire duration of this movement is envisaged as being of several days – perhaps a week or so.

III. *DECAY*

The final movement consists mainly but not exclusively of silence – or more accurately, no sound is to be deliberately created, but sounds may incidentally occur or not as the process evolves. The audience will be encouraged to become attuned to such ambient sounds as remain, for as long as possible.

This is by far the longest movement.

It is, as it were, bridged to by what has happened before, and might be said to be the logical outcome, the final unfolding, of what has previously been worked out and taken place. The process up to this point has been essentially one of *tuning*, to enable better discrimination and enjoyment, by those both within and in the vicinity of the venue and worldwide, of the incidental sounds that are all that will remain. The reverberations of the sounds created by the piece and those that ensue will continue to repeat and expand, declining by the inverse square law previously cited, but remaining at least in principle discernible even after memories fade and after human life comes to an end.

Potentially, the duration of this movement, and of the piece as a whole therefore, may equal the remaining life of the universe itself.

It is envisaged that recordings will be made, but clearly there is no viable playback device that would enable a realistic re-creation of the entire piece in all its many dimensions. This is a piece that needs to be experienced in real time.

Is it possible to define when the end of the piece occurs? It has been suggested that this piece is endless, that it portrays, or enacts, eternity. No such claim can be made. It will have an end, there will come a time when, finally, it is no more. But we cannot say when that will be.

Extract from *Crime, My Destiny*

Brian Marley

While Paula was on tour, wowing northern provincials with the pop-jazz stylings of her mentor Millicent Martin, I got pally with a chap named Tony Lister. The clubs in the West End never failed to attract me, and when I first encountered Tony he was propping up the bar at the Dropp-Inn and spouting witty nonsense to his fellow beer swillers. I'd been living in Soho for the best part of a year, so how our paths hadn't crossed till then I couldn't say. He was extremely well-spoken having, he said, been trained to newsreader standard by none other than Bruce Belfrage, the fabled "voice of the BBC during the Blitz". Well-educated, too. He frequently dropped quotes from ancient Greek philosophers and Elizabethan playwrights into his tales, most of which were so tall they snagged the clouds. He claimed, for example, that in the '50s he'd understudied both Olivier at the Old Vic and Gielgud as Gaev in *The Cherry Orchard* and between the acts had shown them how, counterintuitively, to downplay certain words and phrases in order to maximise their impact – which eventually led to Gielgud becoming a special adviser to the Noise Abatement Society and Tony being awarded the NAS's much-coveted Hush Medal for "services to silence". The more outré his claims, the more I laughed – always with him, not at him. From the outset we were, as the French say, *très sympatique*, and a couple of weeks after we first met, as we stood side by side at the Dropp-Inn's urinal trough, attending to the business at hand, he said, or rather blurted out, blushing endearingly as he did so, that he found me "attentive, intelligent and thoughtful, with a sophisticated sense of humour; the best audience one could possibly have". Quite a compliment, if he meant it, which I believe he did. I may have blushed too. Whenever I joined the scrum at the bar and he caught sight of me, he immediately began to play up – by which I mean *camp* up – his material. In terms of showmanship, Kenneth Williams and Danny La Rue had nothing on him.

Given his air of intellectual superiority, I suppose he was bound to rub some people up the wrong way, especially the knuckle-draggers in the lower echelons of crime, many of whom had had little or no formal education and were strangers to decorum. Often angry and paranoid, too. Naturally they assumed they were the butt of Tony's jokes, which, admittedly, sometimes they were, and it "fair boiled their piss" (an expression one rarely hears in public discourse nowadays but which *my Mr Bushell* frequently employs – everything under the sun seems to boil his piss). When they tensed their shoulders and narrowed their eyes, you knew violence was on the cards.

Notable among Tony's would-be avengers was a scary loon by the name of Sean "Skullcracker" Kilkenny – from, guess where? Kilkenny – who called him to his face a "weaselly gobshite" and behind his back a whole lot worse. He declared, in the presence of at least a dozen witnesses, myself included, Tony too for that matter, that he'd "shut that snobby fucker's yap for good". Not by any means an empty threat. Because of his notoriously short fuse, Kilkenny had a long criminal record. Also a bludgeon secreted in the lining of his jacket. Though he changed jackets according to whim and weather, the bludgeon was ever-present; he probably slept with it tucked into the waistband of his y-fronts. And nothing seemed to please him more than finding an excuse, however trivial, to use it. He idolised Frankie Fraser and, like "Mad" Frank himself, troubled trouble on a daily basis. Only the protection afforded Tony by Robin (baptismally Ralph, I gather, and from Wells in Somerset, not Nottingham) Hood, a loan shark with a fearsome reputation, stayed "Skullcracker" Kilkenny's wrathful hand.

Weaselly gobshite though Tony was, or was said to be by Kilkenny, I soon came to prefer his company to that of all others, my pal Billy and Paula's friends included. Sometimes they'd invite me to a West End show; or to something sporty, such as a boxing match or table-tennis tournament; or – God forbid! – to Les Cousins, a basement folk club on

Greek Street, for an evening of tone deaf hey-nonny-hoing. All of which I politely declined. They meant well and I appreciated their concern, misplaced though it was. They assumed that with Paula in absentia I'd be at a loose end and probably my wit's end. Not so. Most evenings, in need of entertainment and, as Paula would have it in her native brogue, "a wee bitty blether", I found myself among the clientele at the Dropp-Inn, cocking an appreciative ear to one of Tony's spiels.

Turns out my first impressions of him were wrong; he was neither a homo nor an inveterate beer swiller. He merely sipped at his Guinness, ekeing it out for an hour or more and declining all offers of a top-up. In the course of an evening, three pints was his limit. I admired his self-restraint, if that's what it was. Or perhaps he didn't much like beer but felt he had to drink it in order to fit in.

Though I've mentioned Williams and La Rue, Tony's narratives were more akin to those of Irish raconteur Dave Allen, but I'm unable to say who influenced whom, if indeed one influenced the other. Allen frequently visited West End clubs when he was passing through London so he may have caught Tony in full spate. For what it's worth, I thought Tony the funnier of the two.

His inner circle, almost exclusively male, was, however, graced by a few members of the opposite sex, all of whom had to suffer the crude innuendos and insults that were commonplace for woman in that era. They were neither "prozzies" nor "sluts" but when they made that plain they were denounced as "prick teasers" and, obscurely, "pole vaulters". What drew them to the Dropp-Inn, a club that catered mainly to hard drinkers and petty crims (often one and the same thing), was Tony's ability to spin a bloody good yarn out of whole cloth. Also, his send-ups and put-downs of establishment figures and showbiz gods. He was the club's star turn. A few of "Tony's tarts", as they were called, were unmistakably upper crust, and so snooty that, rumour has it, having bought something at Harrods or Harvey Nicks they'd refuse to accept the change the shop assistant proffered, or, if it were forced on them, made no attempt to count it. Apparently, some of them would turn their nose up at anything smaller than a fiver – a Lady Godiva, in the vernacular.

Speaking of nobility, the snootiest of the Dropp-Inn regulars was a certain Lady Steph – that's how she was introduced to me, title but no surname. Of Italian extraction, I thought, from the trace of an accent. A burlesque dancer prior to her social elevation by marriage, though she and her husband preferred to live separate lives, he in the country, she in town. She pretended to be a Socialist and, as if to prove it, regularly out-drank the men clustered at the bar. No surprise, then, that she was stereotyped as a lush and a fag hag. Not that Tony was, as I've said, a fag, despite his affections. Nor, for that matter, was she a hag; amazingly well-preserved, in fact, for a woman of menopausal age who drank nightly to excess and in want of oblivion. "Stephie with the two-ton liver" as she was known – like the chirpy first line of a music hall sing-song. I don't know what became of her but I can easily guess.

 Anyway, although she and Tony flirted and counter-flirted, he was careful to keep her and his other female acolytes at arm's length. It must be said that in the looks department he lacked distinction, being neither strikingly handsome nor interestingly ugly. Quite a setback for most men, but not Tony. Women flocked to him because he was always good fun and never patronising. My pal Billy, who seemed to know everyone, described him as a "spud-faced gallant", which I took to mean he was respectful of his so-called "tarts" and didn't try to foist himself sexually on them.

 Tony had the build of a bear that had stored happy fat for the coming winter. A powerful chap nonetheless; you wouldn't want to tangle with him when he was riled. The first time we went for a drive together, I noticed that his hands on the steering wheel were abnormally large and, from the grip he exerted on it, very powerful. He could easily have made a living as a circus strong man tearing up telephone directories. But no, he had other, more lucrative schemes in mind. Criminal, of course – being a Sohoite that goes without saying.

 When I admired the sensual curves – "inspired by Jayne Mansfield, former *Playboy* Playmate of the Month, as I'm sure you know" said Tony – of the saloon car he was driving (a grey Humber Hawk), he admitted, entirely serious now, dialing the camp down to zero, that it wasn't his. Said it had been "borrowed" from an address in Hampstead while its owner was holidaying in Greece. "It'll be returned, tank topped up, plates swapped back to the legit ones, well before his plane touches down at London Airport. Unless he's an obsessive mileometer watcher, he won't suspect a thing. Anyway, he owes me: I wangled him a job at the corporation, where he's risen like billy-o despite his meagre talents. Sycophants always do." I assumed he meant the BBC, where ruthless brown-nosing was apparently de rigueur.

As we crossed over into Kray territory, he said, "Take this and tuck it away." Under the scant illumination provided by the few streetlamps that weren't broken, I saw it was a Webley Mk 4 revolver, standard army issue, with which I was familiar from my brief, inglorious stint as a squaddie. I checked that it was loaded and the safety catch on – can't be too careful! Was I to use the gun to threaten "Skullcracker" Kilkenny? It seemed the obvious question to ask, so I did. "No," he said. "No need. Thanks for the offer, though." I'd done no such thing but decided not to quibble. "Hoody's boys will give Kilkenny a bloody good hiding or worse when he least expects it. And soon. His comeuppance is long overdue." Then, after a pause: "Such things are usually handled in-house by Hoody, but wouldn't it be funny if he contracted the job out and sicced 'Mad' Frank on him instead?" Apparently, Frank found Kilkenny's brazen hero worship annoying. "What a delicious irony that would be, eh?" He gave a bark of a laugh and, somewhat reassured, I followed suit.

But that didn't even begin to answer my question: Why had I been given a gun? I'd assumed the reason he'd invited me out for a drive *en duo* was for us to get to know one another better, to have an intimate chat out of earshot of his hangers-on, some of whom were habitual gossipmongers and perhaps, on occasion, when short of reddies or in need of a favour, snitches, but when I encouraged him to say more he brought a finger to his lips and shushed me. I managed to stay shushed, though puzzled and a bit miffed, till we reached Limehouse and picked up a pair of black-clad bruisers I'd never seen before. No explanation for this circumstance was given. They dumped their gear in the boot of the Humber and slid onto the back seat from either side. As they did so, I noticed that one of them had a couple of fingers missing from his left hand, the stumps being of different lengths. He gave me the evil eye when he saw me looking, so I turned my head away.

"You're bloody late, Tony!" he snapped. "Still on for the job, are we, or shall I go down the pub instead? It's darts night tonight at the Roebuck. Mann Crossman League finals. Wouldn't want to miss that."

Unruffled, Tony said, "That cheap watch of yours must run faster than Roger Bannister. Suffering saints, how you do complain! We're bang on time, to the very second, and the schedule is as we discussed. Everything's going to plan, and a very good plan it is too. On the drive over, Charles and I went through it, point by point, trying to identify snags or errors. None were found." We had, of course, done nothing of the sort. I still had no idea what this was all about.

"Fingers is the oxy and geli man," Tony said abruptly, by way of both introduction and explanation, "and a champion grumbler, as you can't fail to have noticed. Spike, his colleague, is a safecracker with echolocation skills. The echolocation enables him to hear, without the aid of a stethoscope, a safe's mechanical blocks as he disables them one by one. No safe is safe from him. It may well be that he's more batlike than human – his ex-wife says so to anyone who'll listen. She reckons he was bitten by a bat in his sleep when he was a nipper and is now more rabid than the bat ever was." Adding: "Embittered former spouses tend to say such things." Spike emitted a low growl, though it may have been a chuckle, which Tony ignored and said: "Between you, me, Fingers and Spike we'll get the job done and the hell out a.s.a.p. You've fallen in with the right crowd, Charles. Take my word for it, we're the best in the business! Our slates are squeaky clean: not an arrest, trial or conviction between us. Our dabs aren't even on file." Maybe not, but I couldn't help feeling uneasy. Life was already absurdly complicated due to my entanglement with Frank Blatchington and Billy/2. The last thing I wanted was make matters worse.

But there I was, miles from Soho and the safety it guaranteed. Worse still, by venturing onto Kray territory without permission I was running a risk … although, on second thoughts, not a considerable one. After all, I no longer looked like I did in the "wanted" pic the red tops had published in the days following Junior Bushell's murder. The whippet-thin, clean-shaven squaddie with the buzzcut and psychotic stare was long gone. I now had a self-consciously "arty" beard and my hair brushed my shoulders, giving me, I thought, the appearance of a hip social worker, someone who listened to jazz voluntarily and knew who Allen Ginsberg was. Because of all the beer I'd been quaffing in recent months, I'd also put on a bit of weight, which hamstered my cheeks. But the most effective part of the disguise was a pair of heavy-framed black spectacles with slightly tinted lenses. The effect they had on my appearance was startling. When I donned them and looked in the mirror I could hardly recognise myself. I was confident that even my mother wouldn't be able to finger me in an identity parade. I thought of it as the *my Mr Bushell* look – that of the other "me" squatting in my head, the ugly, foul-mouthed, nihilistic nocturnal ranter who could hardly be more different from equable daytime me. Paula agreed. She found the change so disturbing she made me promise to wear the glasses only in extreme circumstances, i.e. only in an emergency. This outing with Tony was definitely a circumstance with a good chance of becoming extreme. But an emergency? – arguably not. Not yet, anyway. Time would tell. Though I knew Paula wouldn't be happy if she knew what I was getting up to, she was more than three hundred miles away, singing for her supper, and oblivious to my doings. I reasoned that if all went well she need never know.

We drove to the Isle of Dogs at a steady one mph below the speed limit, skirted Millwall Outer Dock, and stopped on a pot-holed road leading to an industrial estate. No houses in the vicinity. No-one about, not even a stray dog. Eerily quiet on the river, too, which Tony said was just a couple of hundred yards away, behind some prefabricated buildings, "darkly flowing with debris, effluent and fish-nibbled corpses". (I wonder where *that* came from.) He killed the engine and doused the lights. "That's our baby," he said, "right there," pointing through a wire-mesh fence to a grubby brick warehouse silvered by moonlight. "As you can see, the warning signs say 'Guard Dogs – Keep Out!' but dogs there aren't and we won't. No nightwatchman either, which is better still. And although there's an alarm system, it's one that even a retard like Kilkenny could defeat. Like as not, it's broken anyway. Okay, chaps, jump to it."

While Spike and Fingers pulled on surgical gloves, Tony popped the boot. They gathered up the tools they'd need for the job – whatever the job actually was, no-one thought to tell me – while Tony used wire-cutters to snip a man-sized hole in the fence. He, Fingers and Spike took turns squeezing through to the warehouse side, after which the wire obligingly sprang back into place. They trotted single file to the windowless flank of the building and turned a corner to where, presumably, the entrance lay. My task? To sit in the car, specifically the driver's seat. The fact that I didn't know how to drive wasn't an issue. "The key is in the ignition," Tony said, "but don't go away, no matter what. And don't leave the motor except to pee. If someone happens by, gets nosy and won't sod off, give a toot. Two toots if it's a panda car – but they don't often patrol the Isle, it's considered too dangerous. Toot three times when it's safe to return to the Humber. Now if, against the odds, panda plods *do* show up and ask what you're doing here, which they'll feel obliged to do because it's in their job description and they work to a basic, easily memorised script, say you've broken down and a pal will be arriving soon to give you a tow. Say you'd been en route to the Ship Inn, just down the road. Act the innocent and don't for God's sake rub them up the wrong way, they'll be suspicious and on the lookout for tells. You do know what tells are, don't you?" I nodded. "Course you do, clever chap that you are!" He took an oily rag from the boot and gave it to me. "Dirty your hands with that to show you've been fiddling under the bonnet." I did what he said and when I handed it back he threw it over his shoulder and wiped his hands on his trousers – workwear, I noticed, of the handyman variety, not his usual Savile Row trews. "Righto, Charlie-boy," he said, "you're fully prepped." I wasn't; far from it. But I felt more at ease than I did earlier. I was confident that, once I'd donned my emergency spectacles, which I just happened to have with me, my disguise would be complete and all but impenetrable. "Back in twenty," he said.

Half an hour later they crept like shadows along the side of the building and paused for a moment, straining to see whether the coast was clear. Clouds had slid between moon and Earth and visibility was poor. I gave three toots of the horn to quell their fears and they hurried over and dumped their gear in the boot. It seemed, from my estimation, to be more kit than they'd started out with, a suspicion confirmed when Spike went back for two more bags, both so bulky they banged against his legs as he ran, causing him to stagger.

Tony nudged me over to the passenger seat, did a quick u-turn, and drove us to a capacious lock-up in, I think, Dagenham. We were there in the blink of an eye. Once inside the lock-up, car and all, we unzipped the bags and revealed their contents: jewellery, guns, stocks and shares, and bundles of used banknotes, Bobbies (twenties) mainly, which Tony quickly divvied up. Though I felt I'd done almost nothing to earn it, I received an equal share. No complaint was raised, not even by Fingers, though he continued to eye me with suspicion. "You did well, Charles," Tony said. "especially for a newbie, which I felt sure you were. Consider your duck well and truly broken. You kept your peepers peeled and held your nerve – easier said than done. Many a wannabee wheelman has bottled it and done a runner mid-job, leaving his muckers in the lurch; but not you, oh no, not you." Actually, I'd become bored while they were in the warehouse and had probably snatched a few winks, but as Tony had sworn us to secrecy I thought the least said the better.

The lock-up was furnished at one end like a bedsitting room. At the other, on a workbench, sat a small hotplate and an equally dinky fridge. The Humber was parked in between, like a room divider. We threw ourselves down on ugly, mismatched chairs and toasted our success with cups of tea heaped with sugar and a smattering of on-the-turn milk. Champagne flutes charged with Bollie would have been more appropriate given our magnificent haul, but, as they weren't available, teacups and tea had to suffice. The sugar rush made us giddy anyway. Tony, a steadying influence, cut through the general euphoria, warning us not to splash the cash around, because doing so would almost certainly be noticed by those whose loot we'd "liberated" (his word, strongly emphasised). "Tuck it away for a rainy day, lads," he said. Which I suspected would be soon – too soon for safety's sake. It rains an awful lot in Blighty; most days, in fact. *Most fucking nights too*, added *my Mr Bushell*. As an inveterate night owl, he'd certainly know.

Having drained our cups to the dregs, we piled into the motor and drove to Limehouse where, on Fingers' instructions, we dropped him and Spike off in an alley behind the Labour Exchange. After which, Tony turned the car's nose around and we headed off to Soho. It was, by then, almost 4.00 a.m. and the moon was still hidden. No-one about, not even drunks too fuddled to find their way home. Almost the only sounds were the purr of the motor and the rumble of tires on tarmac. Tony was more talkative now than he had been earlier, but still he didn't say why he'd given me the gun. Perhaps he thought he didn't need to. Sometimes the most obvious things are the hardest to fathom, even for a bright spark like me.

Odyssey

Meredith Quartermain

You could wander into the library and find a book you'd read twenty years ago, your place held by a bookmark Peter'd printed in the 80s on Slug Press. A bookmark that might say "Move me! I'm burning" or "Wonderful things, brains, my Lord; so good for the roots of the hair." Bookmarks creased and battered or stained with tea. They might commemorate Duthie Books with a line from George Eliot. Or mark the death of Stein scholar Ulla Dydo: "I write any way I can." Or record one of Peter's favorite sayings: "I refuse to worry about it."

You could look along the classics shelves: find Aeschylus, Sophocles, Herodotus, Pindar, Ovid, Sappho. You could find your undergrad Homer, with its marks of your passage. Heraclitus and Parmenides: you could remember Peter telling you about their other way of thinking, remember reading them together. A whole shelf of Loeb Classical Library – you could remember Peter getting those Loebs in the early 70s, furious, they hadn't come in time for a course, from Blackwell's in London, he then writing a letter that began "When I was a boy, my father took me to Blackwell's . . . ," the books then coming by air immediately. If anyone crossed him after that, I'd ask if it was time for a Blackwell's letter.

You could wander along the long wall of poetry – eight bays of books, floor to ceiling, and find collections of all the works written by your friends. You could turn the pages to favorite lines, remember book launches, read inscriptions to Meredith and Peter. The H.D. Book by

Robert Duncan. Collected poems of Thomas Campion, William Barnes. Elizabeth Barrett Browning's *Aurora*. You could browse in Fiction, find novels by Austen, Dickens, Woolf, Forster, Melville, Wodehouse and dozens of others. David Foster Wallace. Joan Didion. Lydia Davis. *The Last Samurai* by Helen DeWitt.

The room muffled in thick walls of books, carpets and double-sided shelving down the centre. A long pine table with space for open volumes and study. On the shelf-edges sleek plastic brackets from the long-closed Duthie's, that slipped under the row of books and held subject tags. Travel, Criticism, Essays, Fiction, Poetry, Art. Philosophy with Aristotle, Plato, Witgenstein, Russell, Foucault, Arendt, Agamben, Walter Benjamin's *Arcades Project*, Peter Sloterdjik's *Spheres*, Jane Ellen Harrison's *Prolegomena to the Study of Greek Religion*.

You could pick up Spinoza's *Ethics* and remember reading it with Aaron Peck – we three The Spinoza Club, rambling through a wild range of our holdings including Diderot's *Jacques Le Fataliste* and Norman Cohn's *The Pursuit of the Millenium* – an unforgettable history of cults and megalomania Peter dug out, the sort of book Peter had to tell you about because he'd read it decades ago and never forgot it, the sort of book the world of ever new and trendy reads easily did forget. Peter led us to other such treasures: Sir Thomas Browne's "Urn Burial"; Melville's "Benito Cereno."

In Reference, you could look up Greek and Latin in Liddell and Scott's or Lewis and Short's fat huge volumes. You could read about Cromwell or hedge-weaving in the 1911 Britanica. Or search dictionaries of symbols, etymology, slang, demonology, plants, religion, science. You could find Turkey in the massive *Times World Atlas* or look up First Nations maps of Vancouver. You could trace the streets you'd walked in Rome on your travel map or the ones you'd walked in London in an old Baedeker. You could sail on *Hakluyt's Voyages* or read the diaries of George Vancouver.

The library cart from Duthie Books, plus three more, stout two-sided beasts on heavy casters, three 36-inch shelves on each side – our compact shelving, rolling up against the wall shelves and holding new subject divisions like Fiction in Translation, where you found Tolstoy, Dostoyevsky, Proust, Balzac, Vila-Matàs, Walser, Perec. Poetry in Translation with Celan, Rimbaud, Mallarmé, Verlaine, Apollinaire, Artaud, Breton. A spillover cart with new poetry that no longer could fit on the wall shelves. A fourth cart with Non-fiction and bound sets: Trollope and *The Arabian Nights*. Full, the carts were so heavy you could barely move them.

In Standard Authors you found gold embossed volumes of Arnold, Byron, Cowper, Donne, Dryden, the collected works of Charles Lamb, *The Stones of Venice* by John Ruskin and many many more. Books Peter'd read as a student and later taught at university, collecting them over more than seventy years. Around the top shelves he'd stowed multivolume hardbound sets: complete works of Hawthorne, Emerson, Wordsworth, Swinburne. He'd stowed notebooks and binders and bundles of xeroxing and all sorts of things I didn't have a clue about he'd been squirreling away over the years.

Chambers of memory and possibility – you could pick up where you left off last year or decades ago, and now thirty years later see how they refract, see what's enduring. *Yes, that's what it means . . . ,* or *No, now with time I see it means . . . .* Not just the words, the ideas, but the covers and pages, the artistry of typefaces, indexes, margins, contents. Were they paperback or hardbound? Soft pulpy paper or crisp calendared? Navy blue cloth with gold embossing or green cloth with red and gold spine labels? Bold colour-blocks with sans serif titles or swank italics with iconic images? On the red-alert missing-book hunts it was always the colour first, the thickness of the spine – did it have a dust jacket? Was it a Penguin? An Oxford?

To have a library, however, you must have a house. To have a house, someone must put a roof on from time to time. Someone must see to the power, heating and telephone bills, the finances and bank statements, someone must see to the yard work, the trash removal, the snow shoveling, the car maintenance. Someone must fix the taps, replace the hot water heater, repair the furnace, clean the gutters. Someone must buy groceries, cook meals, wash clothes, clean floors. That someone became one caring for another who'd forgotten what year it was.

A library cart stuffed to the gills fell over spilling books everywhere. That one had to pick them up, get them back on the shelves, get more of them into boxes. Get people to take them, all the Loebs, Hawthornes, Emersons, Wordsworths, Hakluyts and Vancouvers. All the Célan, Rimbaud, Mallarmé, Balzac, Perec. All the books with inscriptions from all the friends. That someone had to let them go, let them go, let them go. Let them go before they killed her.

Un-doings

Peter Quartermain

I have forgotten how to write

I have forgotten how to write.
We moved, sold our house, now live in a condo, but it's not a matter of orthography. Our house is mostly concrete, not really a house, no garden to speak of, got rid of all the tools.

But no, I can't do this.
I have to find a new way to string words together, I mean learn how to write, physically, as well as thinkfully.

That's a little frightening, everything seems so inadequate to a glimpsed desire. Words, words; words without syntax. What happens to thought, to thinking?

Lou Rowan asked for some prose and this isn't necessarily what he had in mind, nor me. But there is presumably a mind. I wonder what is in it.

Meredith asks, do you want a glass of wine, and I think, no, but realize "yes I do" and have one. Is my mind in a bottle lurking around that bulge in the bottom of the wine bottle, what is that called, does it even have a name, what's in it, can I save it for the next paragraph, will it taste or is it just stale air. Only one way to find out that I can think of. Drink it, throw it out, keep writing, drink it, find out what this lack of focus might be called and invite perhaps some thought.

How many ways was that? A focus is a hearth, the source of comfort on a cold summer's day, and that might bring a place for thought to show itself. We do not have ideas, they have us, but so far in this prose they are staying away, and must be, perhaps, cajoled. But why do I want that to be Cod-Latin when so clearly it is from French, and there's a lack of focus for us all, indeed. In deed writing as a done, as in done with, that is an overall crux. An idle thought to keep the wolf from the pen, writing from the tree.

[2024]

Whatever it was

HAIR. Hairy = angry enough, but whatever.
When I was a kid we'd say don't get hairiated and then I discovered what others said was don't get aerated.

Erk. Is that actually a word. The OED says yes, irk, and if I spell it erk it is surely the same word. But when I was a kid I always took erk as what it was and it sounded so good – you're just an erk – it's a wonderful word and I'm sure I can discover what it really means. Writing it helps, the written word cannot be without sense. The act, the muscle of writing, draws it from and to the body, makes sense. That's how language works, isn't it.

[2024]

In M's Study

I'm in M's study writing things out, warm sticky air on hand.
I'm almost (well no not despair)
confused light
smell? my skin
taste?
touch?
word paper sounds of
utterly illegible oh I can contain
distraction

the window back of me, behind my thinking
on this sunny day, my mind so careless
close to smitten bare of thought

writing from a counsel of despair
wreck the rhythm of thought
but keep the pen at hand
how indecipherable the Buddha on the desk
in my impossible orthography

finding, out the window, clipping branches from the tree
a sapling so quite another venture
another branch of the whatever

how could this possibly be a sauce of delight
a source of delight when if I can make anything
around here I mean legible shows I have something
to say, need to say, something even though
any meaning is a question of inconsequence – a frame

flounder is an interesting word
when one is fishing for something to say

[2024]

Deduction

when I have an adventure
I keep writing then it's its own adventure
trying on the adventure the words lead
nothing follows a plan
it just hangs, I have to forgive it,
an adventure cannot be forlorn
it's just if there is one rule to follow I have to forget it
another adventure cannot be deducible

[2024]

Not a potato of meaning but

writing as a done with
is an overall crux
an idle thought
to keep the wolf from the pen
the writing an abstraction from
the door not
a mere distraction in
or rather out
but never the less the
still of: some hardly witless Now; some
surly curl of tooth creaking
its lip into some
sharp buttress of
dislegitimated pleasure
before some newly minted canard tries
to lose its universe of meant.

Personal geographies: Meredith interviews Peter during lockdown

The Quartermains

On Discretion

M When did you first encounter discretion?
P That was totally out of the blue . . . .
[long silence]
P It has to do with being discreet, there's two meanings at least depending on whether you double the e. Discrete, e-t-e, means unconnected to its surround, has concrete as a kind of antonym.
M Fascinating.
P You knew that already.
M There's what you know and what you're conscious of knowing.
P To be *discreet* is to be reserved, holding something back.
M Mm-hmm
P Not putting your heart on your sleeve.
M Yeah.
P And what's weird about that is to be discreet is to enter an alliance or a pact with whoever you are talking to or have in mind – I won't give away your secret, so it sets up an alliance in which people are separated from one another by their particular knowledge. So when you talk of people knowing, knowledge takes that shape.
M Wow.

P Discretion is the better part of valour, which is to hold back when everybody else is inviting you to attack.
M People's knowledge is shaped by discretion.
P It has to do with keeping things secret or not revealed, if one can make a distinction there. It's a curious word because in the history of it, Pound has a book of essays called *Discretions*, reviews and essays and he has another called *Indiscretions*, or his daughter does. An indiscretion is when one gives away a secret. To be indiscreet is to make public what you shouldn't, like a kid, like when I was a child, Mum and Dad had a séance and on one occasion someone came to the door and I said they can't come because they're having a sitting. I was indiscreet because that kind of knowledge should not be revealed, to reveal it could be damaging.
M Yeah.
P To be discreet is to keep private what should not be told. But *discrete* is something clearly separated out. Sand is made of discrete particles.
M The two discreets are related. One has to do with separate particles, the other has to do with separate knowledge.
P The discreet person doesn't let on what he or she is thinking and therefore can be totally misunderstood. Discretion is a social virtue and in some cases it could be argued that discretion is a class marker.
M Can you give an example?
P You don't let on to anybody, you only let on to the inner circle, I wouldn't tell the plumber. It's certainly a part of Victorian manners, people who are passionately private think certain folk are not one of us.
    You don't bruit your secrets abroad because that makes you available to people, subject to their power, it also makes you boring, do they really want to know all about my printing press. But to publish a book called *Discretions*, doesn't that amount to revealing something, letting the cat out of the bag? So it's a bipolar word both about being reserved and bruiting things about.
M [writing furiously]
P Indiscretion is culpable – that's the connotation, we don't approve of people who are indiscreet even though we love people who are friendly and tell everything.

On Potatoes

M Potatoes.
P For some reason they make me think of flat feet.
M What could make them do that?
P Must have something to do with the sound of the word *spud.* It's really surprising that potatoes are so important, because they're so mundane, ordinary, run of the mill, but like a lot of such things are actually delightful to eat, the versatility of them, a food fairly neutral in taste so they pick up flavours.
M What's the difference between British potatoes and Canadian ones?
P I never ate any Canadian potatoes when I was a kid. The differences have to do with my history with potatoes. There used to be a potato in England called King Edwards – they were imported – a great staple of the English diet.
M Why were they so popular?
P First plentiful, second cheap. They were ubiquitous. They had a nice clear white flesh, not a lot of taste, didn't go mealy. But it was a crop that like other hybrids stopped reproducing. Exhausted its natural life.
M Did people grow them in England?
P Yes but potatoes are North American, and so imported in a way that apples are not. King Edwards kept appearing through the war. Lincolnshire was favorable to growing potatoes. As a kid at school on the farm we tended the potato crop. The prefects organized work groups to hoe potatoes and bank them up. A great excuse to go out into the fields. Child labour, nowadays, but the war got rid of those distinctions since the work had to be done by somebody.

One of the great . . . well it wasn't even memorable was I read about poteen – Irish potato spirits.
M Wow, what are they?
P They're like spirits, a gin.
M Oh, I thought you meant potato souls.
P That was what the revenuers used to go for, the tax men.
M What would they do?

P They would raid because to not pay taxes is to steal from the government, not as bad as forging which was brutally punished.

On the Daily

P A daily used to be something like a char lady who came in every morning and cleaned house for you in the days when middle class houses tended to be large because you had an extended family living in it, three or even four generations, my grandparents on my mother's side had a large house, so did my father's side. But the daily was of course every day and that used to be something people paid attention to. It could be the daily was the newspaper as well as just another form of habit.
M Give examples.
P What sort?
M Production of food?
P Dailiness becomes humdrum very quickly because it is the routine one has to go through to maintain oneself. The daily is, whatever else it is, indispensable. The consequences of paying no attention to the daily are horrific.
M How?
P You starve. Horrific may not be the right word but it's what's available. The daily is that which is essential to your being.
M What happens if you do pay attention to it?
P If you pay attention to whatever the daily is you may transform it and change your attitude to the world. Some things which are daily, hourly, minutely we only pay attention to when something goes wrong. . . . Daily things are something of a habit, the choices I made that were daily. When I was a kid nothing was humdrum. Around six or seven everything is so new that the daily may be everyday, but it was always so fresh and enticing that it was attention-drawing, and I think I only recapture that when I get into various enthusiasms because that's where the possibility is of freshness and newness. Or in trying to figure something out.
M Like a problem to solve could bring something fresh and new.
P Yes, but when I was in the heyday of teaching I loved the irruption students brought into the room because you didn't know what they

wanted to know. I remember classes where I thought I wasn't getting anywhere like a course in technical writing but then I realized I learned a lot about students when they talked, when say they burst out in rage that didn't seem to do with anything but of course it did.

Another kind of daily – I look out the window and see those roses and remember Dad was absolutely enthralled with them and he wanted especially ones which would please my mum. The whole scent of roses, the delicate shading in any given petal. The variety of roses, the richness of what was possible in the rose yard. At the same time he was a veteran of the war and had suffered a great deal, but he loved the history of the rose and its culture and that's another aspect of the daily. For Dad it had to do with an absolute necessity for ritual, walking up the path from the street and stopping at the roses to smell and examine them for blight. There was a virtual ceremonial aspect, not religious but a deep pleasure in the predictable nature of that apparently routine walk up the yard path, the dailiness of it. Things had to be done in a certain order, a ritual procedure and then he varies that in order to make for variety, curiosity. What happens when I do this before that? What happens if I dig up that plant and move it, if it dies, you've killed it with your curiosity.
M The daily has to do with repetition.
P The daily is repeating stuff.
M And ritual is repeated.
P But you can repeat stuff without ritual. Habit is not ritual but if something disrupts things, then you discern it is. I think I put my right foot on the stairs first, I haven't checked. . . . Some people may think the left should go first. Like for the hop, step and jump, I always took off from the left foot. That was a necessary ritual, it also had to do with the belief it was the proper way to do things. A lot of daily activity is like that. You've got to do things in the right order, show respect. Show subservience, like calling someone sir and then expect that back.

On Furniture

M When did you first encounter Furniture?
P I'm not sure I ever encountered it but as a small child I fell over a piece, but that's not a reasonable example. Does one encounter 'a

furniture' or encounter 'furniture'? Encounter 'a furniture' in the sense of having an argument with it?
M I like where this is going.
P It's getting cluttered up in the furniture of my mind. But the furnished is that which is provided.
M So does the mind need furniture in order to move out of itself?
P Do you furnish a house the way you furnish the mind? Yes, there are occasions where I'm renting the furniture of my mind. House furniture is the stuff that makes it tolerable, usable and enjoyable. And the same might be said of the mind because a mind without furniture leaves you without a mind.
M Is there an armchair of the mind?
P A comfy place if it's upholstered.
M A coffee table of the mind?
P Most furniture has a dedicated use but also it is versatile. You can even use a coffee table as a battleship in a game. You could jump up on it and fight pirates. To furnish the mind is what educators do. You give it something to think about or something to think with: logic, mathematics. An unfurnished mind is boring.
M But it could be tabula rasa. Could furniture get in the way?
P That depends on how you feel about pure spirit. But my mind is totally dependent on things to think about. It needs material, they could be abstract but I'm looking at Madelaine Gleeson's painting. Robin was right to say it is a dreamscape. In the sun, you can really see it. It helps to furnish the room, the house and our lives.
M What dreams?
P There are two couples in the picture walking toward a building, males on the right, women on the left. They walk in a tidy landscape with trees to a building that is obscure and might not even be a building but just a wall. Nothing in the landscape is characteristic of anything but evokes a haunting quality, a bit of a cloud, a reflection on water. It is definitely furniture of the mind with its somber light and somber colour. Unlike the big medallion on the wall which is pleasant and ornamental. It does not furnish my mind, it makes no claims on my mind, whereas the painting's details make claims – I discover the ambiguity of sight, there are things in it that have no apparent explanation. The medallion is merely

decorative, whereas the painting evokes another world that can't be completely explained. There is a glow in that obscure building. It's put together to be suggestive. The figures have purpose. The figures are going somewhere but we have no idea where, possibly a gothic haunted house, all kinds of mystery.
M The arrangement of the room arranges the mind.
P The furniture in the room is very unsatisfactory. When I come in I don't think this is a charming or elegant room but it is a usable room, such as the double couch facing the TV. These furnishings tie to the furniture of the room whereas Geoffrey's sculpture could be moved anywhere because it draws attention to itself.
M Can you describe it for our listeners?
P It has a number of things whose significance is not clear but is presumably important in the sculptor's mind. There is the playing-card club repeated across the top and in the two planes that lean against the pillars, the big plane has a large club motif cut through it and the little one has eight smaller club motifs cut through it.
M It has two classical columns.
P Beautifully machined, highly precise. No matter how you place it on a table it is never straight. It resists symmetries of design and placement but has quite strong appeal to symmetry.

On Geographies

M Where does *geographies* take you?
P Back to school because Geography was a totally amorphous subject. It wasn't one. We had Geography classes but we didn't learn anything. We had no notion what it might be. Which has to do with writing and the world.

One of the things I liked about Guy Davenport was *The Geography of the Imagination*. The title promises so much. The imagination has a territory, one you can map. But the book wasn't about that. I thought it would be an atlas of a territory, but that's not what he talked about in a direct way, though indirectly it comes up throughout the book.

A geography is made of orts and scraps. A world you cannot experience as a whole. That has always been a problem. You can't see the whole in any intimate way. A geography could be a survey but my sense of it is rather the substrata, the geology of my thought. A geography of the imagination would show me how it works, but geology of the imagination is wonderful because it can't be described.

M Do you mean Guy's book?
P No I mean geography as a territory.
    When I was a kid in school I liked geography but I couldn't figure out what it was actually telling me. We had maps, and pictures of villagers in Borneo, and bare-breasted women in Ghana, showing me the exotic world we were invited to think of as peculiar. Geography introduced you to new worlds. Later I found it involved looking at maps, finding out whether you can see point B if you are standing on point A. Does the land rise enough to see or not see point B? Only one correct answer. Yes, you can or no you can't. I was interested in hiking and rambles in the Lake District. I enjoyed landscape as a series of interpretive challenges. We'd go to Sudeley Hill and I'd be amazed to see I could look at the map and I could see a particular village, but no matter how hard I worked I still got it wrong.
    On hikes with Mike Mortimore I got it wrong too. I'd find there was a fucking great hill where we planned to go. My whole sense of geography was abstract and impractical. I did no traveling as a kid except by bus to a suburb or the biggest town. The territory was familiar, the geography uninteresting. . . .
    In 1955, Uncle Edward took a school trip to Switzerland. He and the other teacher each brought along a young relative to help with the kids and I was Uncle Edward's choice. We had to navigate from the boat to the train to Paris. I remember vividly in Paris walking past the train engine, a great monster of a thing with SCNF emblazoned on it. I couldn't believe they made things like that in France. I thought the only people who could build trains were the English. But no, all the tracks and trains were made in France.
M Wow.
P I had a little French I'd learned in school, but still wondered as all these people gabbled away in it. It was my first encounter with a foreign language. I couldn't believe the word for *soap* was *savon*. All these

people speaking French, they weren't translating. They were thinking in it. That was such a shock. How do you teach children that? The essential part of geography. That there are radical or minor differences between languages that you cannot reconcile. How can you reconcile *soap* and *savon*?

In university reading Balzac and Hugo in French one began to think in French. Benjamin Lee Whorf's book on language and reality was such an eye-opener, his whole understanding that language stamps your intellectual activity. Thinking in French is different than thinking in English.

On the Political

P The political includes politics and the politic. For a long time, I thought anything that was politic was hypocritical. It carries an air of calculated effect which I thought could by no means be a basis of behavior. It was judgmental, calculating, hypocritical. The calculated, the lack of spontaneity, was to be avoided. You weren't *politic* with your friends.
M Can you really get away from the political?
P In relations to others the impolitic can be a betrayal.
M You could hurt a friend by not restraining yourself – that's politic, no?
P Yes but to behave in a politically restrained way all the time is a denial of love and friendship. A great deal of worthwhile behavior has to do with impulse and spontaneity. To calculate all the time invites an extraordinarily inhibited sense of self. You never give yourself permission to let your hair down, everything is done to an end. You are weighing the effect on others and speculating what effect and modifying your behavior. With those whom I love, I'm not continually managing what I do. I don't call myself up short to avoid certain responses. . . .

P I find it astonishing how easy it is for some to deride and undermine others because they are looking for power because they are so unsure of themselves that they can never appear tentative.

I'm looking at Susan Bee's *Haunted House*. I can imagine myself attacking that painting, as naïve, but it gestures toward how haunting distorts the world we see. We do the haunting ourselves, it's not out in the world.

M How does that work?

P A haunted house is where ghosts appear where things aren't as stable as you thought. A political behavior seeks to avoid any kind of haunting. Politics is a means of controlling and defining those things which would otherwise haunt us. Susan's painting has a strange distorting of reality. Politics wants to remove the uncertainties and threats to stability. You are rendered uncertain of yourself by the haunting. You can't control 90 percent of what goes on in the world politics asserts control over.

M Are there more politics?

P My behavior toward neighbours. A simple caveat we can't escape, I don't wish to cause deep offence, with an obnoxious one we were bullied, with most we are always careful not to offend because that would make life next to them intolerable. But my own politics over all are, don't offend, don't rock the boat, but at the same time don't allow an attack on myself or family. It is impractical to be otherwise so there is a general politic there to do with being polite. [Consults large heavy dictionary.] *Politic*: characterized by policy. I don't state my policy toward people but there is a basic policy there.

M A basic attitude toward the world.

P I did not calculate it ahead but I discovered what I was doing. Politics has to do with the polite, the smooth, the polished, the burnished, a deliberate act or behavior. Dictionary: a refinement of manners, urbanity, which is to say, don't rock the boat. [Slams dictionary shut.]

M You don't approve of what you call political?

P That's correct though I approve of prudence, if being impolitic would disrupt the social fabric.

M What about state politics?

P I'm suspicious of things done for a political party, but as soon as you have two people agreeing you have a party. The only way people can get things done is by agreeing. Political parties tend to be dogmatic about an accepted truth underlying thought. My dad was terribly dogmatic about socialism. When Aneurin Bevan brought in the NHS, dad hated him because he was a dyed-in-the-wool Welsh laborer. He was totally scornful of the privileged classes. My father was so bitterly and deeply opposed to the NHS that he tried to refuse to join. Pay your own bills, stand on your own feet, he thought. Then he got sick with cancer and out of sheer necessity he started to use the NHS. He had to rethink socialism. He had a wonderful time using it when he had a gastric ulcer, the doctor said all he could have was boiled food, wretchedly tasteless, but he could have one glass of Guinness per day and he'd go down and use his NHS prescription to buy a case of Guinness, but he still wouldn't support the Labour Party.

M Do you think politics trumps aesthetics or aesthetics trumps politics?

P Aesthetics come from economic and social privilege. I don't have a sense of a universal criteria of the aesthetically pleasing. This varies from time to time, place to place. My sense of the beautiful has a political dimension. I don't consider the destructive to be beautiful.

M Example?

P Zukofsky. I'm caught up in his use of language. This is an aesthetic delight but I also find his view of the world is actually quite narrow. It doesn't seem to have room for work I find enlarging and rewarding. His only interest is in the intricacy of the structure that he can build through references to history. He doesn't seem to play outside that sphere. AE Conrad would drive Zukofsky nuts. He's a maverick but some of his work is very pleasing. Conrad wants to open things up but Zukofsky wants to delve down into intricacies. Conrad is overtly sexual, angry, scornful. Zukofsky is not going to let the personal appear undisguised. Conrad insists you let the personal appear. That unabashed enthusiasm Conrad has is wonderful. Whereas Zukofsky can feel cribbed and confined. I want to burst out for fresh air. I want the politics to be frankly acknowledged. I don't want it to be so crafted that people say there's more underneath.

[In the Port of Possibility] Interview with Joseph McElroy

Jacob Siefring

Joseph McElroy belongs to a generation of writers that includes Harold Brodkey, John Barth, Stanley Elkin, Cynthia Ozick, J.G. Ballard, Donald Barthelme, and Harry Mathews — all born in 1930, just before, or just after. I began reading McElroy's books after reading the entry for *Lookout Cartridge* (1974) in Larry McCaffery's list of "The 20th Century's Greatest Hits: 100 English Language Books of Fiction." McCaffery had called McElroy "the most important of all 'unknown' postmodernist American authors." What did MacCaffery mean by *unknown*? I had to find out. McElroy was then, of course, unknown to *me*. In a year I read nine of his books, totalling about 4,000 pages. I found no satisfactory answers.

To be sure, the demands imposed by the complexity and inventiveness of McElroy's work deter some potential readers. Nevertheless, I've come to believe that the less that one says about the oft-mentioned *difficulty* of McElroy's work, the better. On this point I side with Kierkegaard where he postulated that "the task must be made difficult, for only the difficult inspires the noble-hearted." Like Beckett's, Proust's, or Nabokov's, McElroy's books aren't for everyone, and, yes, they're daringly original and challenging. There's nothing familiar, easy-to-digest, or generic about them. Wildly inventive, they show a polymath's curiosity for the specialised idioms of diverse disciplines. Urban planning, history, bioenergetics, philosophy, earth sciences, economics, neuroanatomy, Taoism, meteorology, electrical engineering, and more brush up against one another. Yet, amazingly, these idioms function in relation to a strong register of emotional intimacy and family drama running throughout McElroy's narratives. I tested the idea on McElroy that *if there's one thing his books are about, it might be family.* Partial confirmation of the idea came in McElroy's reply: "It's very interesting to me that through this surface, which is American language and history and all kinds of other stuff, you see a kind of substructure or subfeeling of family. Because I think that's true. I wake up every once in a while and find it there, but I don't know that I'm thinking of it all the time."

An unflagging spirit of inquiry and a radically varied syntax are McElroy's signature, elements found throughout the entirety of his work. No other author's work is so thoroughly riddled with questions. Here is a thinker who's skeptical of all the easy answers, who asks hard questions, questions which to countenance redeems an ingrained tendency *I* have to think in settled, reductive terms.

A Smuggler's Bible, McElroy's first book, came out in the fall of 1966. Among the many short-to-medium length experimental novels that appeared that year—Gass's *Omensetter's Luck,* Harry Mathews's *Tlooth,* Keyes's *Flowers for Algernon,* Ozick's *Trust,* Pynchon's *The Crying of Lot 49,* Rhys's *Wide Sargasso Sea,* Cohen's *Beautiful Losers—A Smuggler's Bible* is a masterpiece. Begun in 1963 while McElroy was living in England with his first wife, *A Smuggler's Bible* develops a pluralistic approach to point-of-view and syntax that has remained characteristic of its author's projects for fifty years. Reviewing the book for the *New York Times,* James R. Frakes warned that for serious readers of fiction to overlook it would be to err as egregiously as did the book critics who neglected to celebrate Gaddis's *The Recognitions* and Lowry's *Under the Volcano* when they appeared. Richard Howard, in an introduction that came out years later, called it "a steeplechase of a fiction, taking all the jumps with a style unexcelled by any of his contemporaries."

The decade following the publication of *A Smuggler's Bible* must have been a fury of productivity. McElroy wrote and published four more densely wrought books: *Hind's Kidnap: A Pastoral on Familiar Airs* (1969), *Ancient History: A Paraphase* (1971), *Lookout Cartridge* (1974), and *Plus* (1976). These are each remarkable novels, crafted with genius and originality. Published a decade later, *Women and Men* (1987) has the distinction of being one of the longest and most ambitious novels ever written in English. It centers on a man and a woman living in the same New York apartment building, on their extended families, their stories, on clouds, the future, economics, so much more. *Women and Men* was followed shortly after by a powerful semi-autobiographical novella, *The Letter Left to Me* (1988), set in the aftermath of a young man's father's death. *Actress in the House* (2003) is built around an incipient romance between a New York lawyer and a young Canadian actress, and the murky events in their separate pasts that just might link them. *Night Soul and Other Stories* (2010), McElroy's first collection of stories, included some original stories as well as some pieces excerpted from unpublished fictions. A new novel, *Cannonball* (2013), has as its subjects "the Iraq war, two divers, a California family." It will be published this June by Dzanc as well as reissues of some of his out-of-print books: *Hind's Kidnap* (1969; introduction by Joshua Cohen); *Ancient History: A Paraphase* (1971; introduction by Jonathan Lethem); and *Plus* (1976; to include a poem by Sarah Gridley as an introduction).

After *Cannonball,* McElroy's next published book will likely be a non-fiction book on water. Portions of it have appeared in *American Book Review* and *electronic book review*. For a long time now—about a decade—McElroy has been pursuing the water book, his first non-fiction book project. He has consulted with urban designers, environmental activists, ecologists, hydrologists, and biologists. In fall 2012, he visited Mumbai with landscape architects Anuradha Mathur and Dilip da Cunha and a group of American students to study estuarial proposals. Water has crept to a place of prominence in his fiction, too, with the first chapter of *Cannonball* entitled "to meet the water" (2012, *J&L Illustrated #3*), and several stories in *Night Soul and Other Stories* (2010) centering around that vital fluid which we both are, and are not ("Canoe Repair," "Annals of Plagiary").

The following interview is the product of one meeting and two telephone conversations with McElroy. After I invited him to participate in an interview about Hurricane Sandy and its effect on him, I met with him on November 5, 2012 before attending a reading he gave of his work at the New School. It was the day before the presidential election. McElroy graciously invited me to his apartment, offered me breakfast, and gave me tea. The apartment in which he lives is an open, loft-like dwelling. One book-lined wall of the foyer wraps around his office-studio, and another wall is dressed by a series of encaustic paintings done by Barbara Ellmann, McElroy's wife. These are brightly-colored geometric abstractions, mixing together Mayan and Parcheesi motifs. On the dining room table I noticed a heavily annotated paperback edition of *The Pluralistic Imagination* by William James, several candles (don't forget hurricane blackout), and an old hard-cover of Donne's writings. I was impressed to find that, at eighty-two years old, McElroy appears to be in very good shape both physically and mentally. His movements are swift and firm, his attention probing and well-focused. We discussed the primacy of questioning and dialogue in his work, some water issues, and American politics. Our phone conversations, which took place in November and March, provided the material for the greater bulk of this interview.

In 1952, 1953, 1954, you served in the U.S. Coast Guard. In an autobiographical sketch, you wrote that this was when you "understood for the first time the hugeness of the sea." Now that you're at work on the water book, I can look at your work and see water themes in your earlier work, especially starting with A Smuggler's Bible. *But I am curious specifically what your time in the Coast Guard was like. Can you describe what you remember from that time?*
I should say first, my mind and my plans are full of books that I've put off. I was in two places during the time I was in the Coast Guard. One was a lifeboat station at the tip end of Cape Cod at Race Point, and that was both a lookout station looking for fishing boats that might need help, and it was within about two miles or three miles of Provincetown where the two main search-and-rescue boats that belonged to our lifeboat station were tied up. A picket boat and a diesel lifeboat. They were over thirty feet long, pretty impressive boats. And so when it was necessary to go out into Cape Cod Bay and further to help out with the rescue, often in stormy weather, we'd go zooming into Provincetown and get onto one or

both of those boats. That was the first place that I was in. Then at the end of seven or eight months—partly for personal reasons, although it was great duty and people were nice, I really enjoyed that time—I decided that I really wanted to have sea duty. And so the chief boatswain's mate who was the officer in charge, of our lifeboat station, agreed to have me put in for sea duty, and they found a place for me on a ship in Portland, Maine, the Coast Guard cutter Barataria. So I went zooming up there. And I was on that ship for over a year. I think one doesn't associate that kind of vessel—it's a 311-ft. buoy tender from—sorry, seaplane tender—from the Second World War which had been refitted as a Coast Guard cutter that would specialize in weather patrol. I didn't know that that's what it was, but that's what it was. And so I was just a seaman on that ship, and we would go out for six weeks at a time in the North Atlantic. Once we had a rescue of a freighter that was foundering, but most of the time we patrolled an area of the ocean which would vary depending on the trip, about twelve miles by twelve miles, and radio back all kinds of information about the weather. It was the ocean, but we had also iceberg patrol off near Greenland and Newfoundland. That was interesting. But it was mostly being on the ship and the weather patrol and the people on the ship, and just getting to know how the ship functioned and being out at sea for a long time. So I have a lot to praise about the Coast Guard. They're very good people and the work they do is very valuable. As a matter of fact—I hope I'm right on this, it was always said to me—during the Second World War the Coast Guard lost more men in relation to their total numbers than any of the other services including the army, the navy, and the marines. And that apparently—of course the Coast Guard is a small service and it was then under the treasury department, it may still be—that was because the Coast Guard was largely, as it was told to me, in charge of handling the landing crafts when there were landings in the Pacific and perhaps in the European theatre. Their métier is small boat handling. Of course some of those boats that brought troops in were anything but small. You've probably seen films of them. That's what the Coast Guard did, and so being involved in those landings they lost men. And they lost a lot of men. And so when the Coast Guard is sometimes laughed at by the Navy as being… a safe service to be in, it's forgotten the kind of duty that the Coast Guard provides in war zones. That was part of it. And it was partly the history of it all, and partly the meteorology. There were two professional meteorologists aboard, I spent a lot of time talking to them. The sea itself is just to be lived in and to be looked at, and it was quite different from growing up in Brooklyn Heights where the sea was also important. At one point we had an apartment that was right on the harbor in Brooklyn, and that's what I saw every morning, every evening, and in all weathers. So I think that the sea, the harbour, all that's been very important to me from growing up in Brooklyn. But I had not been to sea until I was in the Coast Guard.

Was it after you got out of the Coast Guard that you began your Ph.D.?
Yes, I kind of backed into it. I said before that there have been—there are—books that I knew I was going to write, and they take a long time. I may have mentioned to you that there is a book that goes back to 1948 and '49 which I'm at last, sort of in tandem with the water book, finishing. It's odd, and I think it's probably better if I don't even speak of it. But the delay in finishing it is not entirely understandable to me. Anyway, that book's getting done. And another one very nearly took me away from returning to graduate school, and I've always had mixed feelings about that. When I was in the Coast Guard, it's 1954 coming to a close, and I had been to Columbia to graduate school, and I had always held out the possibility that I might go back. It wasn't exactly the experience of being on board the ship as it was a sense of it being a transitional, hard-to-define postwar time in America, in the United States. Although I'd never written a novel, though I'd written things all my life, I felt that as somehow launched by or spurred by that time aboard ship and the complicated relationships that were observable at close quarters in a crew. Because of what a Coast Guard cutter does—numbered about 140 people if you can imagine that—I had a society in my head and connected to what was going on in the United States. It was a very typical time, and I think we didn't know what was happening. I think of Norman Mailer's essay book, I forget the title of it now...

Advertisements for Myself?
Yes, *Advertisements for Myself* as expressing something of that time. I felt that my experience aboard the cutter was connected to that. And so I thought what I should do, I should have the courage to do it, was write

that book as soon as I got off the ship, as soon as I got out of the Coast Guard in the fall of '54. But I didn't. Which is not to say that I didn't work on it, but I just didn't write that book. And I think in the long run it was a wise decision because while it would've been great to write bestsellers like Irwin Shaw or somebody else, I think I had a feeling, and not with a great deal of confidence, that the books were going to be in some way complicated, not unreadable at all, but that they were going to be a strange amalgam of experience, of philosophical adventure, and realism, and emotion, and somehow my country also. And so I think I felt that I was going to write what I wanted to write, but I didn't expect necessarily to make my living off of it. And I think that it was probably that that made me not put all my eggs in the basket of that first novel. And so it didn't get written, although it may someday be finished. And parts of it I think have appeared, absorbed, you know, the narratives that I've written. But the book that I thought of that last six months in the Coast Guard didn't get written and instead I went back to Columbia which I enjoyed a great deal and did more graduate work and eventually got a Ph.D. When I left Columbia to go to teach at the University of New Hampshire I had not finished my thesis and I wanted to find out if I enjoyed teaching. I didn't know whether I would or not. And if I had not enjoyed it I would have felt that I couldn't do it well, and if that was the case then I simply would abandon that whole thing. And I always kept alive in my mind that I would write short stories and essays and plays and novels and all of that. So I went back to Columbia and got most of the degree done except the thesis and then went up to New England to teach. I think that it was just as well, because I'm a good teacher. I really enjoy it. It's difficult to teach and write at the same time, but I feel that it's perfectly possible to do that. That's the way that I sort of survived for a long time. Which is not to say that the books beginning with *A Smuggler's Bible* were not filled with anxiety and, you know—will I be able to do this?—and experiment in such a way that I didn't know how the work was going to come out. So that's sort of the way it happened. Over the course of my life I've always run into American writers, very educated people, who apparently feel defensive and sometimes will try to say that if you are teaching, let's say, in a university, that you'll never be a writer. And I think that that just is not true, I think it all depends. It worked out for me, that's all.

I see from Columbia University's library catalog that you wrote your dissertation on Henry King, the contemporary of John Donne.
I did. That's an example I feel, again, of my getting something fixed in my mind, my head, my decision-making powers, that was perhaps not as adventurous or in fact even as wise as what I might have done. I've forgiven myself for it. It's not the same kind of difference between writing a novel, my first novel, beginning in 1954, instead of going to Columbia. It's rather a difference between two subjects. What I did was to write a thesis on Henry King rather than a thesis which I think would've been easier to get published and which would have been a kind of critical biography of the novelist Henry Green. And I mention that because there was a teacher, one of my mentors at Columbia, for whom in a seminar I'd written an essay on Green's nine novels and an autobiographical book of his. I was not myself absolutely sure how important Green was. Imaginative and original, no question. The essay was pompous, and it was over-elaborated, and it needed some editing, but he liked it a lot. And so when I passed my orals, he said—we were talking about my thesis—why don't you get a fellowship and go over to London and talk to Henry Green and do a critical biography of Henry Green. Of course Green became much better known after that, ten years later. I see now if I had done that, that might have had consequences that would have tied me more to the university and to scholarship. I'm not sure. But I didn't do it, partly because I felt that Green was less important than some writers of the 17th century whom I admired very much. And I thought I wanted to write a thesis in the 17th century. But what happened eventually when I got up to New Hampshire was that I became interested in one poem of Bishop King. Then I investigated all the other poems that he had written. Then I got interested in his sermons and to some extent his life. He was Donne's literary executor, I think, or maybe his executor. The connection with Donne was I think probably overly important for me, because Donne is almost my favorite writer. I don't really speak of *favorite* writers—I mean, how can you speak of a favorite writer? But I think that Donne, who is less important than Shakespeare, and less important than Milton, but highly original and complex in a way that I have always felt very close

to, attracted me. And so having decided partly for reasons even of a kind of snobbery that I would not write about Henry Green but I would write somehow about the 17th century, I got drawn into Henry King's best poem, which is called "The Exequy," which is an elegy for his dead wife. And knowing that Green was not a first-rate poet, but a person of some interest I eventually did my thesis on Henry—I almost said Henry Green—on Henry King. So, two Henrys. And the dissertation on King came out. It's okay. I have a copy of it here. I never tried to get it published. I don't think it's all that interesting. People ask about it. But I worked hard to make the subject interesting. That is to say, I know that Henry King is not inherently as interesting as many poets of his time.

I continue to be surprised though that bibliographies of your work indicate no fiction published before A Smuggler's Bible. *Your first novel is so innovative in narrative technique and masterful in its uses of language. Had you really published nothing before* A Smuggler's Bible? *Why did you wait so long to publish your fiction?*

I went to England with my first wife, determined at that point to write a book. Not of that title, but a title which suggested that it would be plural and composed of parts that would be only loosely joined. And that became *A Smuggler's Bible*. And I had real doubts about the rationale of it, because it seemed to me that it might be novellas or short stories that I was trying to push into some kind of connection. But as it developed, I think that the risk was the right one to take. And I think that the sort of precarious coherence among those eight parts was the way I should have gone and did go. But before '62, there was a period of ten years after Williams when I went on writing but nothing that I really wanted to publish or tried to publish as a novel. I think that for a while I was under the impression that you wrote short stories and then you graduated to the novel. And then I realized, thinking of Thomas Wolfe and any number of other writers whom I admired like Dos Passos, that that wasn't so and that the short story was a quite different animal. Although I have always wanted to write short stories and never felt too comfortable writing them, I do go on writing them. And I wrote them during that period when I also was in the Coast Guard and went back to graduate school and Columbia. I think that Columbia had considerable influence on me simply because of the reading. I was quite happy there, and I realized I think there that the novels that I would write would not necessarily be literary, as the publishers liked to call them, but they would be more free and more expansive and would not cleave to the sound of a more conventional American novel. So I think that that was one impact that going back to graduate school had upon me—to remind myself of the options. I remember one of my colleagues in graduate school saying before we parted—I think we never saw each other afterwards, he went to a teaching job somewhere else—he said, "I know that you're going to do something extraordinary, and I think you're going to write books." I was surprised that he said that. Not that I'm humble, but I'm fairly modest about myself, and I was surprised that I had made that impression on him. And I think it was not just the impression of a smart graduate student with whom he would discuss subjects and books—because that's one of the nice things about graduate school. That was about 1954 or 1955. I had plays and poems and the beginnings of novels, and I always had *Fathers Untold* which was begun in 1948 and which I have always believed in. I now have been writing it all my life. And it's only a novel, that's all, it's not the summing up of anything. It is in fact a sequel to *The Letter Left to Me*, but the reader doesn't discover that until about three-quarters of the way through. But I was writing that early. And you can say I was unable to finish it, or you can say I was unwilling to finish it, or it wasn't quite right or something like that. And when I look at what's happened since *Women and Men*, there are a lot of other projects on the table. I guess I've written a lot. But the projects on the table are not finished books. There's one that I began when I was teaching at Queens College around 1989 or so, around the time that I published *The Letter Left to Me*. There's a novel about a changeling and I set some store by that. But it's not finished. And during the 1980s, when Barbara and I spent a lot of time in New Mexico and I spent a lot of time working with a counter-cultural farming group, I have two boxes full of manuscript for a book called *Talavai*, which is a Hopi word for the time of day early in the morning when the Hopi farmer gets up and looks at the fields down in the valley below the mesas and says a prayer about the ground and the crops and so forth. That novel is going to get done some day, and it exists in considerable manuscript. But that's an example of something that I embarked upon with passion. It still exists but I just haven't finished it. Am I someone who doesn't finish things? The nine novels that I have published, and I'd add to that two or three other books—essays and a novella—are not exactly the mark of somebody who doesn't finish things. But I don't feel that I'm like Paul Valéry and reluctant to yield up a manuscript to the publisher. I just think that when it isn't right, you don't declare it finished.

And there's a lot of other stuff. There's a screenplay that I now set considerable store by, which is of the last five years. That's set in Manhattan, although it has an American desert source as well.

There's a libretto which I began with a German composer, and I decided I didn't like his music enough. It's very good, but it's just not for me and it didn't seem to suit the libretto that I had written. I think, now, down the line, Boone is going to score it for me.

So your original question has to do with what happened after Williams. I wrote, I would say, and I read. It was partly a matter of confidence too. I didn't feel that what I wanted to be my prose, my vision, was adequately embodied in my writing.

Was it hard to find an agent and a publisher at all for that first book?

Well, I didn't do much about that. When I was in England writing *A Smuggler's Bible* I sent a couple of pieces to publishers who got back to me in language that I thought was terribly stupid. They didn't really understand what I was writing at all. And these were not difficult, these were early drafts of the first two or three chapters of *A Smuggler's Bible*. And they said, sort of, get back to us. But what happened was that when the book was all done and I'd been communicating with Richard Howard, the poet, who was a friend of mine from Columbia, he'd been very encouraging. He admired *A Smuggler's Bible* enormously and he eventually wrote a review of it. And he was the one who gave the book to Georges Borschardt. And so it was through Richard Howard that I got my first agent. I don't know that that's significant, really. I think especially with a novel, a large bunch of manuscript, that the weight is so inconvenient and exhausting when you do it yourself. And you don't know whether the publisher has put it in a stack somewhere, whether the publisher's read it or the first chapter or the first ten pages, and said, *well, we'll see, we'll think about it*, and then nothing happens. I know young writers now who wait six months. And it's soul-destroying, you know. It's very upsetting, and there may be no alternative. But if you have an agent, at least you have someone who has professional contact with the publisher and can give a description to the publisher of the book and can get after the publisher to decide. Richard Howard was of immense help in putting me in touch with Georges Borchardt, who was mainly known as representing Samuel Beckett and a lot of French writers and some adventurous American writers. He took to my work right away. We had some disagreements later over *Women and Men*, and that's when I went to Melanie Jackson. But I can't say enough for George Borchardt, certainly at the beginning, because he believed in the adventure of my fiction and he thought it had value. And he said, *With persistence you're going to do well and be famous*. I don't know that I would have known about George Borchardt even, but Richard put me in touch with him. So I'm forever grateful to Richard for reading the early draft of *A Smuggler's Bible* and encouraging it and really understanding what was interesting with the book—he associated it with Malcolm Lowry's *Under the Volcano* and some other analogs. But he did put me in touch with Georges Borchardt, so that made a big, big difference. You know I'm really sympathetic to young writers especially now when fiction is harder to place, even though there are many, many small independent publishers. I've got one now. Even now if it's very hard for a young novelist to get read—to get read, that's it.

I want to ask you about the neural, or the neuronal, quality of your writing. Your autobiographical essay "Neural Neighborhoods and Other Concrete Abstracts" seems like a substitution of 'neighborhoods' for neural 'networks,' perhaps. I've also read a claim, somewhere on the Internet, that your writing has the capacity to makes the neurons tingle. That phrase in particular resonated with me as being very true. Very broadly, where do you think that comes from?
Well, you know I wrote this book *Plus*. And I've been interested in neuroanatomy. And... but I'm not exactly a nerd. I think I always felt that science and technology, different kinds of science, were part of the language that we speak in these times. And I was never really interested

in writing science fiction, and I think that *Plus* probably is not science fiction, it's some hybrid, transcendental science fiction type. I don't know what it is. But I think I often felt drawn between, divided between, threatened by a division that is in us as well as in me, between the organic, normal observer of the world, and someone slightly crazy. And by that all I mean is that our ideas, our perceptions, our ways of understanding the world and putting that into words—all of that is, seems to me connected to a brain. But I don't really mean that, it's connected to networks in our whole physiology, not only upstairs but the whole body, that embrace the autonomic, and embrace the very powerful, and embrace the animal and the chaotic and the very mysterious. So, not to turn this into a dichotomy exactly, because we think in twos, we think maybe too easily in terms of two. I still felt that tensions in me that were part of my vision and my desire to speak were drawn between this kind of straightforward, ordinary-citizen kind of person with a body, and this other being that is connected to, that arises from, the just unbelievable complexity of the brain, the mind, the body, and that is not understood. Its power is used. Something like that. I think it's in *Lookout Cartridge,* I know that it's in *Women and Men* but I think it's in all my work, I think it's certainly in *A Smuggler's Bible,* but I think it's in *The Letter Left to Me,* where the young man, or the boy if you will, in the sentences, in many, many of the sentences, most of the sentences—is both here, and moving ahead. He's both here and in the future. And I feel that there's a sense in him, not only of the civilized, articulate teller of the story of a letter and how it got taken away from him *twice*—he didn't *learn* the first time, he let it happen the second time—that he's telling the family story in a way, which is partly about bereavement and partly about freedom. He's telling this story, which is maybe the most straightforward of all my stories—although I'm told that it's complicated, and I think it is complicated—but I think that's represented by his being here and now in the present, but also always pushing ahead into the future and being in two places at the same time. And I think often in the syntax of the sentences, that he's these two—not these two people—but these two forces, and that there's a hidden force which is driving him which he doesn't understand himself. And, in fact, I'm getting back to that in the 1948 novel which I'm at last

finishing now. And I'm making that a little bit more articulate and explicit than I have before.
Mm-hmm.
So I don't whether that makes any sense. But I think... for lack of a better metaphor, I think there are these two forces, and that the unseen force which is not really like D.H. Lawrence [*laughs*], it's more like Henry Adams, I'm not sure. But it's something which is complex, and it's sometimes representable in terms of neurophysiology and representable in other forms. And... I also do want to mention that there's a guy in France who's written about me named Yves Abrioux. He has an essay about *Lookout Cartridge* and *Women and Men* in which he says that what is unusual about me is that I have given body to the mind, or given body to the mental, or given body to the brain, or given body to these complicated processes that could be called neural. I don't know what I would think if I read it now, but that's Yves Abrioux. When I read it. I thought, he's got it, he's got a line on me. It's nothing that I would want to make more articulate than that. But something about the novel being or giving body to the mind.
Yes... I think that there's something mysterious and evasive about that question that may be hard to respond to fully.
No, I think it's an important question, but I don't feel really able to be more articulate about it than that. I think maybe the novels are articulate. What happens in this other novel—actually there are two—there's *Voir Dire,* which is a big long one, which goes from 1991, but this other one that began in 1948 called *Fathers Untold,* I think it maybe gets into that neuronal chaos that one protects oneself from, but one also wants to enter and make use of somehow. We'll see, I don't know what the book will be like.

I want to ask you about something one of your characters said about reading, about books. Generally speaking, I think we regard books and education as empowering, as liberating. But for Michael Amerchrome of A Smuggler's Bible *it has become something like a burden or a hazard. He says, for instance: "I gave up reading because I was paralyzed by quantity." Also: "the further I read, the more thinly I felt I was spreading myself." Did you ever feel this way? Have you, for instance, ever felt it difficult to negotiate the dialogic relationship between reading and writing?*

You mean to become a reader rather than a writer?

Yes. I'm thinking about the opposition between the two acts. I mean, whether or not Michael Amerchrome speaking there is you *at one time. Or if you felt that: "the further I read, the more thinly I felt I was spreading myself."*

Yes, I think that's part of me. I think it's part of me. I'm tempted to generalize about all writers, but I better not do that. I knew a writer in France called Léonie Bruel, and I liked her a lot. But she believed in not reading anything. Because if you read—you know it's bullshit, but—if you read it's going to destroy the voice that you have. She was an extreme realist, there was nothing experimental about her. She wrote about coal miners in France. That sticks in my mind because when we were talking I realized that, maybe to a fault, I read and read and read and read. And I'm interested in books. And then later I sorted it out and I figured that one's consciousness is always sorting things out, and what comes to the surface or at least what you can access to work with is never all this learning that you have, this reading. But I think that there was a time when I was maybe drawn between would I write or would I—well, I would always write—but would I write, or would I be maybe a scholar? Undoubtedly a scholar writing, but not a writer in the same sense. And I think also whatever that feeling is that the character has, there's a fear of being flooded. And it's most of the time a very modest fear and it doesn't affect me much. I was just thinking today, looking around at the books here in this apartment, that I'm so lucky, you know, *I'm so lucky* to be a reader and I'm thinking about how other people spend their time and waste their time or at least spend their time, and I'm so lucky to hear these other voices, you know, to be exposed to them and to let them help me think or sometimes help me escape. So I don't have really more than a kind of chaotic reaction to your question about the character. There are times when I have felt that way but mostly I just wish I had three or four lives to not only give all the time that I want to to writing, but to do all the reading that I haven't done.

[*interviewer laughs*]

But not because I think I ought to or that I'm going to be on the $64,000 question or anything like that or even to be able to talk to Boone about it, but just because it's such a pleasure, you know. And that's why it's parallel to my amazement about how people lack curiosity. I'm sure you run up against it all the time, you must. When young people say have read this and that, this bestseller, and often I have not, I always take down the title and maybe I'll get around to reading it. But another part of my mind is saying, well, you want me to read this thing or that thing, but have you read Dostoyevsky? Or, have you read Plato? Have you read the really important stuff? And usually not. And I make my peace with that. I don't get angry about it, I don't preach. But I think that the books that we have are so incredibly valuable and that the life that we have is not long enough to be acquainted with them that it's kind of a frustration that some of these acquaintanceships I will never make. When I was visiting Jeffrey Allen's class at the New School on Wednesday, we were talking a little bit about books and how important I think it is for writers to read. It may be perfectly true that writers are driven to writing by painful experiences, by experiences of love or of betrayal, or who knows what, and they're also driven by other things. I think that they're driven to write, or they write as they do because of the reading that they're doing at the moment. I think we're very literary in that regard. My connection with that is very sophisticated, because I've read so much and I've thought so much about the kind of voice that seems natural to me. If it is an amalgam of other voices, if it is influenced by other voices, it's been somehow compacted or turned into something else. But I know that it's not only a deep consciousness of myself, of someone joyful and someone hurt, someone historical, and someone impulsive, all of those things. It isn't only that Joe. It's also a lot that I've read. And so it may be that when I'm anxious about spreading myself too thin, whether it's reading or writing, I'm aware of how much there is that's accessible to us in books. Of course, I'm always always hungry to meet people. There's also that, you know. So I'm not sure I can give you a very coherent statement on what Michael Amerchrome said.

I think you already did, Joe, I think you already have. I want to ask you about the Internet. Particularly I'm thinking of one book that appeared in

2010, you might have heard it, by Nicholas Carr, The Shallows: What The Internet Is Doing to Our Brains. *As you began to use the Internet, I presume in the '90s—and I know you use the Internet like everybody else now, and on a regular basis—does the Internet make it harder to get into a mode where you're immersed in your work? Is there a pull away from that interior world of the novel and of the book?*

No, I don't think so. No. Although I think that the world of the novel, the world of writing, the world, if you will, of a structure made out of words and thoughts, is to some extent an escape. Just as it is always a healthy escape from other things in our everyday life, I think it's an escape from the Internet. Do I go and check my e-mail too often in the course of the day? Yes, I do. And I've noticed that when my Internet goes out occasionally, my first reaction is neurotic. And then my second reaction is to think, "What the hell." [*Pause*] So I think—I mean, I have a new feeling about it with the Petraeus case, but I've always known that somewhere, in some fortress or some cyber-concept or habit or organization, all my e-mails are kept and saved. And this is a little bit like thinking of all the things that I've said, as a teacher for example. I've been told by a couple of people who interviewed me that I was one of the few interviewees they knew who answered their questions eloquently and even in [*laughing*] in fairly complete sentences. So I guess I speak more or less articulately. And I think that would be what I would find if every word that I ever said in a classroom for thirty-five years came rushing back at me like a flood. I probably would find that it wasn't all that bad, as I find when I look at a book that I wrote a long time ago with some apprehensiveness and find that, well, it's not all that bad. But I think I feel that now about e-mail. There was a time fifteen years ago, maybe twenty years ago, when someone, a friend of mine, criticized me for long e-mails, for treating the e-mail like the old hand-written letter, or the typed letter. And I think it's true that I do. I don't know that that is really using too many words. I think what it is is being warmed by the e-mail. And since I'm someone a little bit paranoid who wants to go to the post office when he finishes a letter and mail it, although one doesn't do that anymore except for bills, I feel gratified that I can send a substantial e-mail to you, or to my son, or to Marie Barrientos, or to any one of a number of other people who are in my extended circle. My daughter. And it goes right to them. Whether they read everything in it, I don't know. E-mail and the Internet I know are not the same thing. But I think e-mail has been very comforting to me, as if I can speak to someone in written down words and I don't have to wait for three days to imagine their receiving it. So I think that's been good. I don't think that I'm much interested in the cyber alternatives and potentialities, like what Bob Coover is into and always has been for many years. And that's I think a regard in which I'm not a postmodernist. I'm probably a postmodernist in an uneasy, unresolved, still negotiable quality of the reality that my books are about. And I'm probably a postmodernist in that I do go in for parody at times, and I'm quite literary. But I think basically I'm not a postmodernist. I think I'm just not too interested, in spite of what I said that Monday night [during the reading McElroy gave at the New School]—*what could happen?* is what I said and *what could happen?* is a very important question—in spite of that I think that the answer to it doesn't go in the direction of Coover (cybernovels). But it goes in the direction of a kind of discerning, philosophical, more commonsensical approach. What is the most interesting solution to the dilemma that you find yourself in at this point in the story? What's the most interesting solution? Not *many* solutions, but I guess one, you know, the one that's more interesting than the other. I think that cyberfiction has opened up the possibility of many endings, parallel work, maybe a little bit like what Burroughs was talking about. But I'm not interested in that. I think it makes me uneasy. And I'm not really confusing this with the Victorian novel's double-ending, like in *Great Expectations* and then in our day *The French Lieutenant's Woman*, where you have two endings to the story. Two are like one. But cyberfiction conceives of there being innumerable endings, and the richness of this, of the imagination, is all very well. I guess that's healthy. Maybe you keep it to yourself as a kind of energy that you can use. But to turn what used to be the text into a limitlessly openable and multipliable experience is not too interesting to me. In fact it's not interesting to me at all. And so insofar as that is connected to the Internet, the cyberpathways, I guess I don't much go along with it. The advertising and the information, most of that I think is a drag. But I do use Google. And there was a long time when I thought, "I have to go to the library"—you know, I go to the Columbia library, to the

NYU library, I go to my own library. I like doing that. But I realize that as long as one is careful and thoughtful, Google has an astonishing amount of quick information. I use it.

Your forthcoming book, Cannonball, *is about the war in Iraq, among other things. Can we expect that it will reflect how warfare has changed so much technologically?*
I doubt it. It's as much about the narrator and his relation to his sister and a family on the West Coast as it is about the war, how he gets into the war, how he goes there. By a very interesting turn of plot, he briefly but unexpectedly returns to the war, and the powers I would say of evil in this book are under the impression that he's returning to the war because he's going to hook up with someone whom they want to find. Then they discover that that's not why he's gone back to the war. He's gone back to the war for the most vague, powerful, existential reason in the world. It's just to be there among certain people. And so it's about him and his development as a person. He's young, very young, and it's about his family, so it's a lens on America. It's not really like *Ancient History*, but it has a quality of *Ancient History*, come to think of it. And it's not about photography, but he's a hack photographer and he's in the service as a photographer. What he manages to see with the camera becomes something of an issue in the book. The book is also about the dynamics of a family that's coming apart and not coming apart. It's also very much about the way the Christian religion has been misused by the right wing in this country.
I can't wait to read it.
Well, you'll get a chance, soon.

In 2003, you asked Harry Mathews whether writing should hurt. Your asking of that question may have been due to the fact that Mathews's texts can appear opaque and nonsensical. Now, as you know, some commentators, some of them very astute and others of them inept, have called your own work difficult. How do you respond to this question, which you yourself formulated: Should writing hurt?
Well, I think the answer is yes, it should. I think it should, I think there should be an out-of-control feeling projected by the work. Let's say we're

talking about fiction, though I think the water book has some of it also, that's non-fiction. It's that we are tipped out of ourselves into something a little larger than ourselves. It's partly connection with other people. It's partly thinking, it's partly regret, it's partly imagination. And this is a painful process. I think that there is an awful lot of writing that in many, many different ways is safe, and I wouldn't feel this if I didn't feel that I am guilty of this myself. Someone wrote me an e-mail the other day saying, would you contribute to an anthology that this guy's putting together, or some essay that he's writing. He wants to know why writers write, so tell us why you write. I'm not going to do that, I don't want to do that. First of all, don't trust a reader when the writer tells you why. [*laughs*] And second, there are just so many different reasons. But as I talk to you right now—it's all a metaphor of one kind or another—I would think that I write partly in order to remove the cloak, to remove the veil, to make myself naked. And by that I mean to tell as much of the truth about what I feel life is like as I can. And you know that doesn't mean telling the story of my mother growing up in Freehold, New Jersey, it doesn't mean Brooklyn Heights, it doesn't mean autobiography In the usual crass sense that people mean when they say, Is your work autobiographical? It doesn't mean that at all. It means a stripping away. It keeps me going. It's hope, it's a kind of wonderful gift and hope that I have, a hope that I can further strip away something which I'm hiding from myself about what I've seen. I think everybody has it if they could just let themselves reach it, whether it's in this art or some other. And I didn't mean to imply that in Oulipo or any other work of Harry's—highly sophisticated, often very funny work, he's got a wonderful sense of humor—that he was shielding himself from something that I would call raw, or more real. I didn't mean that at all. I was simply asking the question because I think it's a question that Harry's work tends not to ask. And that's okay too. It's an issue. As I say, it's to do with hope and a feeling of being blessed, although I don't know who would be blessing me. But I feel blessed because there's more of this to do all the time, I feel I haven't finished. It's not exactly that there is a particular book I need to write. It's that the process of stripping away goes on, and it's not only exciting and scary, but it's interesting, it's just interesting.
That's really inspiring and beautiful, Joe.

In the late nineties you were asked to give descriptions of what books have left the greatest impression on you and why. Your response focused on Nietzsche's The Genealogy of Morals, *Siegfried Giedion's* Space, Time and Architecture, *Alexander Herzen's* My Past and Thoughts, *and two other books. What were those other books?* Great Expectations was one of them, and I wrote a couple of paragraphs about that. Sentimental as Dickens as, it is still one of the great novels and quintessentially a novel because of its sense of snobbery and emotion and a whole life. It's just a beautiful, wonderful book. It was also the first novel I knowingly read. I was a sophomore in high school and my teacher was a very good teacher and also the music critic for *The World Telegram*. He was a man of many parts. He was the first one who helped me to understand that reading might be analytical, that you might read this book not just to be carried along and then come to the end, but to see the parts and see the interaction of characters and to extract an idea or two. I may have understood it in my heart somewhere, but it was the first time that I understood you could do that. I've reread it many times, and then I've even taught it a couple of times in classes.

    I believe that the fifth book was either Beckett's *Molloy* or *Swann's Way*. Both of those I love. Proust as you know I'm very deeply touched by. I taught the whole of Proust to a graduate class at Temple. It isn't just *Swann's Way*, it's the whole thing with its flaws as well. But it's characters, the characters that are so extraordinary in Proust. There are characters who are not drawn the way a lot of American fiction draws characters, characters who are drawn with long ruminations about the ideas they have.

David Segal edited Hind's Kidnap, *and he died shortly before* Ancient History *came out in 1971. You dedicated* Ancient History *to his memory, and I wonder how important he was to that book. Its first line is,* My luck you're not here. *In some ways, I can see that first line almost as addressed to him. He would have been editing the manuscript you were submitting...*
David was certainly one of the most imaginative and cantankerous and adventurous young publishers around. I think what happened was that

David read *Hind's Kidnap* and bought it for Harper's, then went to Knopf. After *Hind's Kidnap,* I wrote *Ancient History* rather rapidly and David accepted it for Knopf. We talked about it and he did some editing on it, and we talked about future work. And then when *Ancient History* was in production David died. There've been many editors of mine who've died: Timothy Seldes at Harcourt Brace, then a woman at Harper & Row, then David Segal, and then Alice Quinn at Knopf, and several others. including Lee Gerner and a whole slew of editors at Knopf. But David died suddenly and it was startling to me because he had certainly been such a supporter of my work and so, as a kind of last minute token of my sense of him I dedicated the book to him. Now it's coming out again. But that first line doesn't really have to do with David, because I wrote that when David was very much alive. It's just what it is. It's about the relationship between the narrator and the Dom character.

Now I'm thinking about that piece from a different angle, because I'm writing a piece on Garry Winograd's photographs. I'm working from the catalog, and I'm going to go out to see the photographs at MOMA in San Francisco. I think very much of that time, the late sixties, '69, '70, and so forth, the demonstrations, the cultural upheaval. Some of it Norman Mailer's involved in, although I think maybe Mailer's position in that novel is overstressed by those who like to find keys to things. But Mailer was part of it. I think of that period of time in relation now to Winograd's photographs and the seventies. You know, his sense of crowds, of the vectors of people's eyes looking in different directions, things on the verge of disorder and chaos, but somehow the photograph *composed*. Which is one of the great things that he did with his street photography. It ran its course, and I think he got a little bit tired of some of those compositions and, whether wisely or not, he left New York and went West. But I think of that time, the sort of turmoil that infiltrates *Ancient History*. At the same time that you have the individual story of the narrator and his country friend and his city friend, where there's a kind of focal reduction of simplicity, there is also a sense of the disturbances going on in the nation as there is in *Lookout Cartridge*. That's a time when David Segal was very helpful and understanding. It's a book that was criticized by one of the publishers at Knopf saying it's the least of my books, because I think it doesn't develop character and place quite in the way that he thought was appropriate. But I think the book is original. It is what it is, that's all. But there was a time when David Segal was on the scene and then suddenly he was not there, and I then went through a succession of editors. And it was a time when I was trying to rather quickly capture a feeling in the United States.

I'm very curious about the relation of Kierkegaard to Hind's Kidnap. *In "Neural Neighborhoods" you wrote: "Between Kant and Kierkegaard, my hero set out -- to dekidnap places, persons, memories, memory, himself, and a real child different from himself." You saw these two philosophical figures, Kant and Kierkegaard, as present in Hind's quest. Kant is very present in that book with the distinction between using people either as a means or as ends in themselves. That's quite explicit. But—*
I don't know that I can really add to that. I think not only Kant, and not really mainly Kierkegaard at all... Kierkegaard had certainly a presence in my feelings for a long time. But I think generally in that book a deeper acceptance of philosophical language and the philosophical enterprise as being acceptable into the process of fiction. I believe I write quite dramatically and I'm capable of writing scenes and narratives in which physical life and setting are all fully rendered. But I do believe that people think. And I do believe that the whole history of philosophy, which could be summed up as the need of questioning and which leads into abstraction as well as into concrete examples, is, as Barthelme said, part of our focus, part of our energy. And I think in *Hind's Kidnap* somehow I was willing to let ideas surface in a more explicit or abstract way. I think mainly in the narrative, not so much in dialogue. You get to *The Magic Mountain*, then of course you've got it in dialogue, and it's a question of whether that works or not. I think in *The Magic Mountain* it does fabulously work, but there are an awful lot of people that hate that book because they feel it turns away from drama and physical life and the reality and psychology and so forth. I don't. But I think that at the time I was writing *Hind's Kidnap*, I was willing to move away from *A Smuggler's Bible* in this regard: that philosophical illumination was an analogue for feeling and for trying to wrestle things through. And so maybe some of the prose comes out as being more abstract. I'm not sure. But I know that I felt this in *Ancient History* and I certainly felt it in parts of *Women*

and Men. And so I don't really want to put it more explicitly than that. But a way of saying it is, with Barthelme here, not at all to rule explicit philosophy—the crystallizing of our problems into philosophical rumination or discourse—not to rule any of that out as a verbal texture which is directly related to the life of fiction. One way of understanding that is simply to have characters who think, but that isn't exactly what I mean. It's as if there's almost a biological ground which runs through what we call our experience. And that biological ground can take many forms. It can take the form of the austerely rendered scene as in Hemingway. It can take the form of the passionate communal history of the South, for example, in Faulkner. But it can also take the form of a quest for understanding. And so it might be possible to pick up as I think I did and as I am again the conflict between the aesthetic and the ethical which Kierkegaard talks about in *Fear and Trembling*. And he means by *aesthetic* something a little bit different from what I mean in the water book where I'm talking explicitly about art. And it seems to be surfacing as a quite explicit theme in our culture right now. I find it everywhere. But it's always been in my thinking that the aesthetic and the ethical are much much closer than traditional philosophical categories have supposed. And I think of the many urgent, pulse-rapping distinctions that Kierkegaard makes between the aesthetic life, by which he means a life of pleasure and intellectual pleasure quite different from an ethical life, which is a life of risk and choice, like Abraham for example. Still, there is in Kierkegaard a model for what developed into my thinking and my uncertainty about differences between aesthetic experience and ethical experience. I think that they grow together in my thought and in the water book and I think in *Women and Men* is partly due to thinking provoked by Kierkegaard but by a number of philosophers, not least Spinoza.

As for the Kant in *Hind's Kidnap*, as David Segal, who was trained as a philosopher at the University of Michigan pointed out, there is the idea of there being no end in itself, or the idea that it's very, very difficult to identify an end in itself. I think that came from Kant. And when I say came from Kant, I don't mean I lifted it. But you find something in a philosopher, and it confirms something that you feel in an inchoate way. It becomes a little more crystallized, a little more clear.

I'm reading Either/Or, *and that book is very much about the distinction between the ethical and the aesthetic as well. So there it is in his first major work.*
I suppose so. I guess I knew that once, Jacob, but I don't remember [*laughs*] now that that is so but I'm sure it is so. I think *Fear and Trembling* was important to me also. In some sense I felt I was risking a kind of writing that would not be raw enough... and that persists now. I feel that there are some unspeakably painful stories, if you will, that I have yet to tell. And not that I'm too literary or too cultured or too sheltered or even too shielded or too screened, or my writing is too screened—no, it isn't that. It's just that I feel that there's some ultimate unveiling of not horror exactly, but of depth and pain that I haven't come to yet. And I think of what Kierkegaard says somewhere about trying to be another, which has always been interesting to me. I connected it with suicide, and I connected it with the creation of character. Somewhere he talks about the knight who doesn't make a commitment or doesn't make enough of a commitment, who, I think he says somewhere, *has no inclination to become another.* I think I've always been torn between the need to project into others and in a way to lose myself in order to create character, and on the other hand to write in the first person and to strip everything away as Beckett does sometimes, to strip everything away to some me that I haven't yet been willing to face. So I think there is Kierkegaard, too.

And you have a good memory for it as well—you do.
Well, [Paul] Valéry, in a short prose work called *Monsieur Teste*, at one point has Monsieur Teste speak honestly about remembering what we read where he says, "what could stick did." "What could stick did." [*laughs*] So I fall back on that. Who knows whether I can claim that I've been deepened as a person by all the books that I've read, even though I may not remember them too well. My friends are kind enough to tell me that I have an amazing memory. I hope that I have a memory for feelings and for people as well as for what I read in books. But my sense as I'm sure your sense is too, I've heard you talking about all that you've got to read, is of chaos and disorder and anything but an orderly memory. I think Freud would have something useful to say about this—we

remember what is useful to us. I think memory is much more complicated than even Proust presented it to us as being. Full of accidents. Reading has certainly been very important to me. Why wouldn't it be? At its best it's the work of let's say a writer who is trying to boil it all down, what he or she knows, and I want to know about that. I want all the help I can get.

Two Poems

Tony Baker

1.

"On top of the piano
a little fine dust" .

Crossed paths of walkers
on a towpath, unknown

to each other , each
to their own place their

           own populace .
Out of earshot
a vista of distant quayside cranes
comes to an arrangement with itself .

Can we agree on this Maurice
that on top of the piano
        is a little fine dust ?

I'm only saying .

Pax, let's take it on trust, my friend .

*(Originally made with a piano accompaniment derived from the
fiddle tune, Cooley's, for the memorial to Maurice Scully in Dublin, 2023.)*

*

2.

Across the neighbouring field the rain
slants down . Four horses stand , snort , seek
no shelter . The physical

      earth folds back upon itself
to the point that nothing matters any more
than this enduring wait, barbed
      wire through grass or grass
  grown back through .

So skint we are , unwavering
echoes , as it tries and tries

   & tries to speak .

REVEALED, REVEILED
a suite for Randy Hayes

Joseph Donahue

I

Buddhas in cellophane.

In this world, things that appear most
clearly conceal other things,

or stand between, or float over, or slip through,

as the tree blocks out the mountain,
or the blaze of the sun consumes
the surface of the lake.

Waves lost in their own candescence
but the shadows of the waves –
hardly more than ripples,

they seem to seethe.

The title page of a book is folded over.

Sleek and smooth through a slit
in the skirt, the transvestite's thigh.

Clarity proclaims hiddenness.
The seen is never complete.

Petals floating in a votive bowl
conceal the translucence of the water.

The divinities are wrapped in cloth,
bound with rope around waist,
neck, and hands, like hostages
in a film about terrorism.

In India, drying linen covers low shrubs.

In Ellensburg WA, a young girl in a T shirt
--faded image of a reggae singer—
leads a blind horse through a parking lot
cluttered with pick-ups and Teepees.

She is looking down, appears solemn.

In the Netherlands, a bike draped
in dried leaves leans against a brick wall.

In Mississippi, a cabin is devoured by ivy.

In Bangkok, Buddhas packed in peeling tinfoil.

In a summer palace in Beijing, the statue of
a dragon is contained by chicken wire.

In many, many, places around the world
architecture is lost behind scaffolds.

A section of Westminster Abbey.
The dome of a mosque in India.
A huge gateway in Inner Mongolia.
In Amsterdam, a wall of the Magna Plaza.
In Rome, the tomb of Augustus.

So too several floating restaurants in Hong Kong.
Squibs of piping and planks under huge sheets
as if a magician were about to make
the whole world disappear.

A lion. A woman. A tank. A fluttering bird.

There is a partially obscured receptor dish atop a palace.

In Mozambique, mask on his face,
a man with a weed whacker.

In Seattle, a hooker pulls a vinyl miniskirt
further down over her upper thighs.

Thailand is a huge outdoor chessboard at night.

A smiling guard stands among chess pieces,
wrapped for the night in clear plastic,

though it seems a few of the
thigh-high black pawns are not.

In Rome, pop singer Andy Williams,
at night in a plaza, before huge columns.

Massive black door, spectators held back by ropes.

Movie lights turn Andy Williams pure white.
So, too, the hairdresser who walks behind him,

So, too, the umbrella the hairdresser
holds over the head of Andy Williams.

In the lobby of a Beijing hotel, stone
and marble in elegant swirls, on the floor
by the staircase, a large black urn.

The urn is behind the piano,
but from this distance the urn
seems on top of the piano,

as if it held the ashes of
a pianist or of a singer.

Three jackets hang on posts of
a fence around the Forbidden City.

In Jackson Mississippi, at Dr. Duck's bait shop,
a sports utility van blocks out the sign
on the bait shop that begins:

Pawn Shop Cash Loans on Guns.

In London, behind shop glass,
rabbits dangle by their back feet.

Their upside-down bodies are partially lost
in the reflection of the street on the glass.

In the reflection is traffic,
a corner shop with letters reversed,
and possibly the shadow of
the photographer of all this,
shade heightening the clarity,

Randy Hayes, ghostly, on the glass.

II

e Eterna

If the word is a word, in whatever language, there is an e (long e) in front of it, *e eterna*. No x after it although an "ex", some last abiding frazzle of Latin, flashes in your brain. *Ex eterna*, out of, away from, eternity, *ex eterna*, or is it formerly eternal? Then, as the flame of white off-center left on the canvas comes towards you, you feel you can't stay in the uncertainty of *eterna*. You feel that, as you study the letters, the white light is getting close to you, whelming your vision. Turning to it, you can see that the sense of its being borne towards you had been confirmed. A figure carries it, a running child, bearing aloft a torch, a torch about to be handed on to you in a tragic relay you did not know you were a part of, the very torch carried by generations of runners through the hilly terrain of Asia Minor, a torch lit from the fires of Troy. Perhaps you are the lucky one who will carry the torch into the city. What city? The one where Clytemnestra waits for Agamemnon to return? This is the fire seen with a woeful shudder by the guard on the wall at the opening of the *Oresteia*, the guard who foresees what will befall and so is struck dumb. Since the messenger, here, is, in modern times, no more than a lampstand, some stay from grief is available. Still, there is word to be delivered, word that the world's most civilized city has fallen, that it is now gone, and we are still living the fall of Troy, but the word is not to be delivered till the spell is broken, the spell that imprisons the messenger in this painting, perhaps by Hermes himself, who more often leads souls into the eternal. Our world is a canvas chockablock with emblematic stuff. Greyish blue takes on a tone of finality. The table lamp creates a shadow figure on the reflected whiteness of the tabletop. The figure seems less like a god from antiquity than a vodun doll. The eternal may be a curse. Such speculation is belied by the calm and solidity of, at the bottom edge of the table, a book, and on or under the book's cover, a gondola. And a name, Monteverdi. The curse of the eternal gives way to dreams of a holiday, of sight-seeing in Europe, of a first-rate summer production of a popular opera. The book is leatherbound. You can feel in your fingers the pleasure of its heft, perhaps beneath the cold stone archway of a public monument with winged cherubs holding a wreath. Have we already read this book? Perhaps we are drowsy, and the book has been set down beside the bed here in this atelier overlooking a canal. Perhaps when reaching to turn off the light, we will find that our hand is that of Edith Warton or Henry James. And what have we been reading? The closed book is forever closed. Unknown. But there is the open book in the upper right corner, open to the title page: La Secunda Part Della Geographia Di CL Tolomeo.

III

as much as Randy said Randy as much as said

Randy as much as said: I have a philosophy about the image. As the image darkens. Or brightens. Or becomes clear. Loss is always involved. There are images behind the image, and they fade. They are lost, yet these two things depend on each other. That's all. The visibility and the beauty of the image, and then the image that must be taken away. It's simple, but it takes a long time to understand. If I wrote out my philosophy, that is what it would be.

Randy as much as said, on the anniversary of, for me, an overwhelming death, each grid is a veil. Each grid was in appearance a wall of photographs. What Randy does is take photographs, hundreds, thousands, of photographs. He travels around the world, he walks around a city at night, bars and graveyards and convenience stores. He takes pictures of places and people in places and then he pins some of the pictures on a wall, in careful rows. Then, since he is a painter, he paints some extraordinary scene on top of them.

    Randy as much as said: Do you see that knotted curtain in a room in China, where a figure in a dark corner has her face in her hands and then you slowly notice a photographic image is there, where the paint thins, ghostly landscapes, portraits, hidden from view, they break in on her world, on your world, like a memories, like a piece of a past life, but a life that isn't yours. You never get to see your past lives because you don't live in one of my paintings. But then, a much-missed past life can vanishes as soon as its seen. Maybe the lives that compose the veil of the grid is hers, the woman in a room in China. Maybe that's why she is grieving so deeply. Her life, her memories of all her lives, are gone in the brilliant colors of the present, yellows, blues, in the gold, in the green.

    Randy as much as said: The paint on the photograph is also a veil, a veil that varies in its densities, in places almost translucent, a gold or blue wash in places as thick as a drop cloth, the realities that the photos render seems beyond any gaze forever, and yet one knows it's there, and if the painting were destroyed, could be seen. The painting defies us to destroy it, Randy said: When I paint I like to ask myself how badly do I want to see a hidden image of the world?

IV

Crucifixion in Silver at 10:19

    The wall. The cross. The Christ. A silver-grey glance. All seems stamped out in metal, not so bright a metal as to be ornamental, a few shades too grey. But after a moment, a warm a grey – is there some blue in it? Some pink? Traces of dawn or twilight mixed in? A moment more, the grey turns resolutely industrial, the tint of a lid or a bumper on the hull of an ocean-going ship.

    A shadow between the crucified and the wall. The cross as if made in elementary school arts and crafts. Beams cut from cereal box cardboard. They recall that the vogue for breakfast cereal comes from the revivalist zeal of the 19th century. Then they were covered with wrinkly silver foil. Perhaps the cross is evolving into serious metalcraft, a sword, a shiv, something pounded into shape. The clock on the wall may be a photograph, the one photographic image in the painting. As such it attracts attention. It achieves priority over the icon, so much larger, beside it.

    Washed out, pale, almost swallowed by the wall, the clock dominates the setting. It's Baudelaire's own crucifix, dividing time into the stations of the work week. At first the clock challenges the cross, historical time's triumph over ritual time. But the new, secular temporality reveals itself to be just more of the ancient and ongoing agony. The clock is the cross all mortals hang upon. The hour hand sunk in the ground, the minute hand a cross bar, the second hand the centurion's spear.

    Th time notation, 10:19, 25 seconds short of 10:20, is at odds with gospel accounts. So, too, the rendering of the execution. The arms of Christ have been broken off and removed. The hands are still nailed, at the wrists, to the cross. A red glow marks the left shoulder. There's a touch of red on the cross behind the head.
It is strange to see those two hands like two gloves hung up to dry on a clothesline, the hands that calmed the seas, that multiplied loaves and fishes, that drove out the moneychangers, that broke the bread, that healed the centurion's son.

V

No Cover

A window frame, huge squares of glass, nine all together, three rows, three per row. The bars of the window frame are white, though they absorb the color of the two sets of bright long neon tubes on either side, one hot pink, the other yellow.

Between these two zones of color, the exotic dancer, looking down, her head framed by the top middle window square. Her body is caught between the yellow and the pink. The pink hand rests against the window crossbar. But her left hand that picks up so much of the yellow is open palmed, upraised as if pushing against the glass, her thumb hidden by another window cross bar.

In the mirrored door behind her, her reflection, back of legs, shoulders, back. Her ass is quartered by two bars of the outer window, the window she dances in, window looking out on a street in New Orleans. A man stands outside, eye-level with her feet. In profile, his shoulders half turned, as if he's about to walk away.

The window onto the street is the first frame within the actual frame. The nine panels of glass within the larger window are a grid over the dancing woman who looks down from the top center plane. Th mirrored door frames her. The wall may also be mirrored. The bars of the outside window seem to be reflected within the window where the woman dances.

It may be a mistake to see her as dancing. She may just be stripping. Her knees are together, to one side. Both hands raised in front of her. One hand might be waving. the other seems to be deflecting or fending off or exerting control over the viewer, clearly not the man who has already looked and seems to be turning away. (So then, no one else but you.)

The center pane cuts off her head and hands and most of the legs below the hem of her very short black skirt with the top part of the outfit that would cover her belly and breasts, the straps, one forming s small loop at her hip, as the whole top half has folded over, crumbled in what could almost be called her lap. Her breasts are covered by a black bra with black string binding. Since she stands at an angle, her right breast is more exposed. It pours down into the black cloth. Her left breast, turned directly towards you, has touches of blue paint that sharpens the focus. Her eyes are hardly eyes, rather, smears of black paint that intensify her dominance. You feel the stripper sees you, though you cannot see her seeing you.

The eyes are the window of the soul. But here, you are not allowed to look into them. Alone on a street in New Orleans, you look up and feel lost. A speculation is gathering, or rather, a bewilderment. On the breast so provocatively presented, are letters composed of electric bulbs, though many are burned out. The message is nonetheless legible. They spell out the name *Christ Jesus.*

Sound, Sound and Summary
—"mu" three hundred fifty-first part—

Nathaniel Mackey

    We found ourselves tight the day
  no number would attach to. Date-
  less days' turf it was we were on or
                                                       it
  might've been, must've been.
  Reciprocity's feather fell adumbrat-
    ing the break of day... It was all
                                                     there
  for us to take, soon-come sonance,
    see-thru sonance, all pomp and
  circumstantial command as a wasp
                                                     re-
  galia, snake handlers happy to be
  stung. We'd've been better off not
  being, the feather's fuse implied or
                                                     in-
  sinuated, itself an enlistee into eve-
    ry lost cause. It was all only what
  it was, tautologic conscript, crib, crypt...
                                                        In-

sofar as this was what it was we were
    singing, the world, our singing said, old
and mean. "So said the song, so sang the
                                    sing-
er," went our refrain, belief borne close to
    the belly, belly borne as breath and be-
leaguered strum. Of all things, bluegrass
                                    ban-
joes and guitars readied our way, snuck
in among our sitars and our sarods, Celt-
ic harps not far behind. We stepped away
                                    from
    wobbly barstools on the edge of plan-
et Earth, subsonority having its oblong say…
    Thru the would-be window of soul we
saw lions, wild dogs and hyenas feasting on
                                    wart-
hogs, a bloody savanna wet with warm en-
    trails, the eating-alive of everything of
which we too, we saw, were a part, the lion's
                                    jaw
God locked or God let loose in the first
    place, retributive grapes one after another,
multiple and singular, each accretively oth-
er… Subsonority waged war for the soul of
                                    some-
thing some said had no soul, heads atop
    bodies too big for them, short on mind as
well. All it was was Nub's illusory lack of
                                    in-
side eyes we confronted, so many things
unraveling raveling otherwise. We were
up against or gone up against by exactly it,
                                    date-
less days' turf subsonorous too, subsolid the
    closer in we went, a closer walk we took

        not yet knowing what closeness was, holding
                                          hands
          as if skipping rope… Subsolidity had a way
          with us. Its way, Mr. and Mrs. P said, the
        it of it all up on and over them, a thing in of and
        apart from itself. The word *quantum* they had
                                                had
          some history with, as had we all, but this
          wasn't that, no matter how related it was,
        a cousin thrice removed or twice removed if
                                          at
        all, a cousin once removed at best. Was the
        way its own or simply extrinsic, some random
        way, the way it had with us, we wondered, Mr.
                                        and
        Mrs. P notwithstanding, before after after
          intermittently, after before before… "Before
        after after, after before before," said Sophia,
                                          re-
        joining Mr. and Mrs. P, exactly so, calling
        herself a squint optimist, knowing by that
        we knew she spoke for all of us, we of the
                                          long
        view. Subsolidity had a way, not its way, the
          latter an implication of solidity subsolidity lay
        at odds with, the pre- or the proto- state what
                                          hope
          was left rest-
        ed in

•

  No time soon would we be done with
  the way it had with us, no time soon
  would subsolidity lift or congeal. We
            stood
   on a cliff looking out at fireworks
   as far as we could tell, fireworks over
   glistening water. We stood looking
           at
  starburst over a bay and then smoke
   lingering after, squint-eyed and
   elegiac, no moral bend as far as we
            were
  able to tell and no just arc as yet. We
   stood squint-eyed, optimistic anyway,
   smoke a requisite complication we
            fig-
  ured, we could barely keep from
  laughing, not give away the joke… It
  was all we could do not to give it much
  thought or too much thought, the way it
            was
   having with us one of many or itself
  many. Sums, no matter what, were al-
  ways beyond us, as if some last incre-
  ment could never be accounted for, "as
             if"
   itself that increment perhaps, "per-
   haps" an even further increment, an
   elapsed equation forever to be made
            up
  for. It was all one to us even so. We
  had said it before and we now not so

said it as thought it, wanting not to or
                                              not
wanting to, careful not to give it much
   thought or too much thought, a loop we
laid back and let have us, a way with us
                                                    if
nothing more, nothing less… So it was
   all one to us we said without saying,
thought without thinking, a toothpick, at
                                        best,
between our teeth, not to be noticed.
No time soon would we be done with
   it or it with us, subconscious as much as
subsolid or subsonorous, what there was
                                            there
and what there there was, all one to us
we kept noncing, not saying. Equally so
we sang without singing, nonsonancing,
                                          bits
of melody caught in our throats. The ex-
   quisite mereness each of them seemed was
exquisitely not, a lump of cud more likely
                                       or
a wad of chewed-up linen, the muses'
   draped unlikeliness we would draw no
closer to… So went what was now a nonsong
   of relinquishment or a song of exhaustion,
                                      sum-
mation's tour de force or its cri de coeur,
if not both. Not since nonce met nonsonance
   had it been so clear, so bluntly come thru
                                        al-
beit see-thru, "all one" professing harmony
   or indifference or both as we mutedly bit
and chewed on toothpick wood, homonymic
                                          splin-

    ters of "would" fanciful or not, all one to
us which and whether it was or it wasn't con-
ditionality itself, a nonsolid interstice we
                                                  took
  solace
in

                _____

      A glimpse was all we got. And then an-
other. Glimpse by glimpse as up a knot-
ted rope knot by knot, glimpse by glimpse
                                    by
glimpse. To see was to be knotted so,
   "not since" crossed over by "no time
soon." No time soon would sum not
                                  ho-
monymically splinter, ever amount to
  more than some… One weathered
it nonchalantly, blasé, toothpick against
                                one's
  dry lower lip, snugly stuck between
two teeth. "Lobsters in a boiling pot," one
  averred, "no toilet flushed into the same
                                sewer
  twice." On a day without number so
went the art of oratory, offhand, low-key,
  rope the new wood, as in *Give them*
                                 e-
nough and they'll burn themselves,
grim take on the interstice conditionality
                                  was
  taken to
be

(13.vii.24)

    In the realm of number as if we'd
never left the polls were saying this and
saying that, many of them and each
                                    with
   many tongues, depending on whose
    ear alighted on it and whose mouth,
   the many indicators said to alight
                               or
have alighted, no one ascertaining
   which but quick to surmise. It
was Friday the thirteenth a day late…
                                  We
   were looking to be looked back at,
   birds' eyes caught catching back,
    the birds' migratory witness wherev-
er and when, granularity's precinct
                                  prev-
  alent everywhere… We no sooner
saw the incumbent under fire fired
   up in Motown, Orbán and the former
                                  prez
   in Florida chanting, "NATO day
   done," than we saw a "second amend-
   ment solution" attempted on the
                                  lat-
ter in Butler, PA, Nub sublimity's
                                  dimin-
  uendo in
white

    Come Sunday we were back in
    Low Forest, the numbers not yet on
our side but also not yet against us,
                              the
    poll that would matter four months
    away. Heat and humidity met
us on our return… The leaves in Low
    Forest were sweating, so hot was
                              it,
    the world, it seemed, cooking
    slowly, an airy broth atop a low but
    persistent flame, a low simmer…
                            All the
    old and new habitations of soul had
    a "say" in and had to do with it,
"words" whose reckonings we picked
                              at,
    parsed, picked apart. An ellipse com-
    posed of birds' eyes twirled us on
                          a hill-
side and in a meadow and up on a roof-
top, a rough, wobbly spin rumbling like
                            a ma-
    chine unevenly
loaded

―――――――――――

   Red the new white, diminuendo in
     blood the old and new white, an ellip-
se's oblong wobble. The stretched or
                                the
   squashed or the elongated circle, a
     pitched or a porched Pagliacci, wav-
ing home… "No time soon" and "not since"
   the two foci of the ellipse, crossed eyes
                                  or
   crossed legs or star-crossed embarka-
   tions put away as if gone, the it of it
   bent whatever way and bent back but
                                  final-
ly not it-
self

Three Poems

Eléna Rivera

Considering Circumference

I said "House on fire!"

Seagulls just flew by—

I asked "Are you listening? Or, circling around your own thoughts?"

Sometimes I think, "that's enough"

Do you still believe we orbit around it?

I'm careful with my wings

Aren't you ever concerned about heat?

Success in the world will not give us more of ourselves

There's drying yourself out, you know turning yellow

I was consumed by spirals on the terrace

Can you want the kind of heat that will smother you?

I hid in a deserted building until it was destroyed by fire

> *Let's dance put on your red shoes*

The wax melted on the counter and now everything slips

In the middle of reading Chekhov, I lost the thread

We let Helios regulate time

The machine is star, all that light

You're just jealous because you don't have my tan

"Under the sun" I wonder "can we have radiant crowns?"

Give me one drop of water and we'll come out of the dark

This golden house is it here or elsewhere?

It will burn, and this time it won't just be the poor

> *Let's dance put on your red shoes.*

The Logic of Lines

After Amy Sillman's 2007 oil painting "C."

I'm hanging in the midst of colors by my black lines

You surround me like a clear surprise so that I'm not

sure where you begin and I end, except for the lines

that frame the light in the distance, in surroundings

that color our vision (did I mean to say 'clouds?') I have

no answers just lots of elimination—I have only your lamp

on my side, the dipper, as I make one error after another

trying way too hard to cover up all the destruction

Meanwhile I end up on the shelf, unable to get out into

the refrains of my body, a mind that "repeats in my ear"

You are in that courtyard with me playing and sounds

ricochet—relieve me of my memories—I see the struggle,

the ghost told the poem, make it and unmake it, then

scrape, "sometimes you need to be able to tear things

apart to realize the result," more and more elimination,

scrape hard to step forward into bands of yellow, pink,

gray practically hidden in dramatic colors of the exterior

Essential and listening to both languages — I fell off not

being able to connect to ancestors—my amor turned

on by the crashing going on outside the window, can't

ignore one mark, "I do have a" *serious* "vibe, but ... I ..."

Most quoted material by Amy Sillman

Of Circulations

instrumental in keeping language alive

a wedge between fields

steadfast in going back to a time now present in space

as it turns out was at a Buddhist center in my teens

she was surprised to hear

the house was cold, damp, spare furnishings (what one would call

"boxy")

sitting crosslegged was something the girl tried to master

and living in community

there was little responsiveness in other quarters

"in muddy waters"

what does an enlightened person comprehend

I wanted out of the relationship

wore black, smoked cigarettes, sweated as I walked (still sweated then)

waited for the school-bus to take me

played the part of the Queen

and spoke Spanish in that *Chamber Music* one-act

the role assigned cracked under pressure but not completely

that was always the question, caviar vs freedom

what circumstances allowed for the world

the word I was longing for

riding out on an elephant was the natural response

unless stuck there with it in the room (boxed in)

not quite the way to describe what I was feeling

doubled over in pain

the dream: to ride out of the binary

the pelican flew over the empty beach

"caution is required in a difficult time"

what do they say about the color of sheep

wanted to exit the fixed and return whole, not old

for a while fed the horses at the farm

thoughts fly if they ...

if the words are yours (but wasn't sure of that)

forever following

the muse built inner reserves and kept a low profile

maybe the heart's in the right place but what about us in the penitentiary

all of us in apartments, towers, behind doors (what you would call "boxed in")

mattering so little (in the bigger picture)

slaves of thoughts and convictions

"caution is required" especially when watching movies

keep an eye on the mind

fables, facts, paths

can torment the outcast with more images

walking down to the beach

still no documents of that time

until a kiss opened floodgates

at the threshold something always happens

Four Poems

Aidan Semmens

In passing

between these lochs and hills
whoever comes, whoever goes,
whatever livings make their way,
the stones stand still

embody the long moment
of ritual transformation and resistance

the shoreline, the horizon, the instant of death,
mists that descend and depart,
all those edges that divide the known
from the unknown, commonplace
from the strange, process
and precession

where the thrashing restless tide
hits habitable landfall, scours
the bedrock of its sandy cover,
throws salty spume a mile inland
on moving air, tossed with curlew,
jackdaw, redshank, heaves up
slippery spoilheaps of tangle and kelp,

threatens undercutting of the overhang,
erosional slippage and crash, a periphery
where destruction and creation engage

gun batteries, lookout posts, command centres,
cinemas and toilet blocks splinter and rust
on abandoned shores and hillsides
or do duty now as sheds and byres
settled into the landscape
like every derelict homestead

tokens of a different mundanity
transactions of the rite

beyond the sound familiar forms
of cliff-edge and moortop, unreachable
as if mythical, hidden, a memory
not quite to be trusted

light on cloud and water
constant change
with the appearance of stasis

A partial history of peat

From satellite or pilot height you see
a continent of smoke, a mountain range
of Himalayan scale poised over Siberia,
concealing its own shadow
on the smouldering land below,
a tundra land awaiting redemption
from undead zombie fires.
Where families carved out

precarious livings from under heather slopes,

that peaty taste of whisky, smoky on the tongue,
is the delicious taste of death.
It tastes of forests felled and timber burned,
flayed uplands gasping from the plough,
of bog lands, sphagnum moss and ling
concealing dark ponds fringed with cotton-grass,
of wetlands drained of life to make up ground

for oats, barley, wheat, asparagus and fine grazing,
improvement of the forest swamp, a rip
in the fabric torn for development, progress,
growth. Here's a coin-bright birch root,
remnant of primeval forest, hunting-ground
of a mythical warrior princess. And here,
carefully cut wet then dried, the sculpted
modernism of a neatly stacked bank

laid in a herringbone pattern to repel
wind and rain, where a whiff
of peat smoke smells like survival.
Ash and oaken piles, aerobically preserved,
support remnant traces of willow walkways,
paths across the bog, a place
to stand ankle-deep and watch
bright jets carve trails against the sky.

Cities of the lost

In an unmapped stretch of tundra
four times zones east lies
a city so secret it has no name;

zeks built the baths and furnaces
of a polis poised on columns
above the permafrost.

It is perhaps for us the children
and grandchildren of the nomenklatura
to relate these remarkable truths.

In the darkness of a polar winter
the wire and watchtowers are tidied away,
no more hungerstrikes in the mines

but pride in the scale of suffering,
rust-shattered shells of factories
and rotting lumbercamp huts.

From marshy forests of cedar and larch
to lakes among birch and pine
the people have their shamans,

keepers of memory, ritual, exile;
penal servitude must serve
for socialists and other old believers.

No exit by road or railway is available,
just a dam in a canyon blasted from granite,
spring snowmelt slipping down the spillways.

Between the lines

We were authors of our own downfall, they said,
written on notepads, old envelopes, shopping-lists,
in margins of our favourite books, afterwards
typed up, set in stone or hot metal,
on billboards, signs by the roadside,
painted finally in the blackest paint,
taller than human height, on the wall

that divides the land of brother
from brother, tribe and sub-tribe, you and me.

Consider all the things we never write
or amend with the imperfection of memory,
the tunes you can't quite place,
something that must be overcome
like the rows and the whisky,
the clatter of pool balls in the rack,
the nameless asteroids and satellites,
constellations we'll struggle to identify,
the streets we walked down before, perhaps

long ago, and how they correspond or don't
with the colours and shapes badly printed
on the mental retina. Or recall maybe
that evening we crowded off the bus
to wrap fingers round warm greasy newsprint,
sinking ourselves in the scent of chips and batter,
or the night we stood in the metal chill
of a Finnish freighter's open deck
and watched in vain for a glimpse of the aurora.

That day we walked the length of Oxford Street,
elbowed by strangers, and gawped at the lurid display
of shiny commercial detritus, bought nothing,
while Soviet jets flew secret missions far from home,
US agents sowed undercover seeds
of assassination in newly democratic nations,
lovers sprawled on worn grass in the royal parks
and somewhere an unseen star maybe blinked its last.
And how this evening's easy reportage

and the assumptions of history, pretending
to a knowledge of hidden events and the arcane
chaos of chance, fall into unacknowledged gaps,

relationships of which imagination
can make only spurious sense.
Like all our ancestors we expect
annihilation or, exhausted, seek
the blissful insulation of unknowing,
relief from daily expectation of calamity.

We all have our territorial imperatives,
the unwritten spaces that separate column from
column, head from text, lines on the map
that thicken like arteries with age,
cutting down flow and presaging the end
of someone's days. The passage of time,
you say, brings its own hilarity,
but it's a dark passage where no one whistles
or reads the rushes from our own correspondence.

Poems

Simon Smith

LITHIUM

Without shadow, feathery, without shade – side on the profile silent & invisible, like a blade to the air. Burns on contact. The silted & choked rivers, dead & oxygen gone – suffocated, rotting fish, rotting silver on the bank or quayside. Mercury & other heavy metals. Traces. Without.

For the digital asbestos: to follow up, to collect & spy, copy – the pattern of life, the R9X six blades, laid open a body steaming & shredded & stumped. The World to be, to be read as text. Data. Fug. Knowledge siloed, reflected in the photomask. Without doubt. Just out of earshot.

Fixes my brain & mood, powers my phone, the fusion fuel. Total eclipse. Also, a kind of gift. Hearing the wind through horse chestnuts cupped to my ear with my hand, white as noise, cut with other elements. The ICBMs falling nowhere tonight. Reality is data. Dead & for nothing.

The memorabilia, notes, bills, chits, chaff, receipts, rubbish, dust, muck. Let's say there's a hierarchy – the orange flowering, then spreading blind light, a detonation observed 800 miles distant, away, sand melted to glass, to a paperweight, arms without strength. Melted. Outliers.

Believe your ears, your eyes, your nose, your tongue, before – in crystal form to take the edge off, for a gentler World. The shadow army improving light or recycling the water. The gleaming shimmer of flies. I am in the silicon & the silicon is in me. Body quivering, the one on target.

VISION embedded, for good. All eyes. The complete interrogation system: the tiger chairs, the cell bosses, focus groups, the works, is to know the right people, the folk – information, bits, the fragments, predictive, from Life into Real Time, through the fourth wall, light folding.

Is to lick the analog, Real Life – the moment's edge. The sight of the deer not the deer itself. The World to be read as text: wing tipped with the final call. The 'New Managerialism' hungry for data. You are the semiconductor, the World to be, to be read, as text affects invertebrates.

In the hollow of a wave, the back of a wave, the freighter & junk glide silent, float illusion. Look– the shadows are long, the days are blue in little anagrams or petals. The lung, in the unanswered questions of 'of,' the words lift together, light skimmed. Mylar, film. One at a time.

Delicate as brushstroke, devastating as tsunami, swirling boiling dirty grey waters. 2004. Between the Great Curve & the Great Wave. Echolocations. The Dead of grey sludge. Like a blackbird, the song high & startled – suspended perspective – locked in the integrated circuit.

Fata Morgana. The boat straightened in the current, linear, analog, dark matter between. How you prove not being there. Father levitated in the glowing dark performing triage. Shipping container floating above him. Image out of control, arms flailing. Over the horizon operations.

The light, the cracked diamond, the lighthouse. Every now & again – of anamorphic illusion, soft enough to cut with a knife. In foreign lands don't drink the rainwater; in all the countries don't drink the rainwater. Feeling nowhere, thinking nothing. Love & the forever chemicals.

GRAPHENES

White on white stained off-white residue. Powdery. Shadow. White. The unique snowflake, the singular Lichtenberg figure, the magnetic field, the magic in the fold of "what if" – all on film. Like to like. Latticework. Whipped back to the sloosh, sometimes to the fade. Sometimes.

Through the use of pencils & other applications to form, graphene, the white noise of all I'm receiving & saying. In shadow, in carbon. Subject to direct sunlight. A snowflake – ever fading & dissolving patterns, unique, particular, anonymous, contingent, miraculous. Gone.

The sine in the sign, sky's blue churn, a single cell thick, air moving the air moving. From snowflake to signature, that curve & trajectory. Rub the surface lightly, silvery & light entanglements flutter & twist, falling through falling. Sketch or drawing, arc & turn.

In small quantities. To ice melt. Cursive, hands linked in "like". & pixilated. How to discharge the charge & love the love with the capital "L". The form of electrical breakdown, if we treat the angels badly in transition between worlds – to touch fingertips, flip wingtips. If.

Shush, what's your safe word, 'backlit'? & wobble. Signs the thinginess, shows up in guesswork & patterning, grapheme, of battleship grey. Gull up like a kite. I'm writing the code, a half step, the journey safe. To show workings out, the apparatus, one thin film. The Golden Section.

Allotrope of carbon in a single layer of atoms. Diamond's distant cousin. When you hear the music in the World, the possibility in the impossible & what slips away to the non-existent. We exist on the Cloud, alongside the angels – we were transitioning all along, God gone.

The God gene in the God term, liminal & edgy, the singing in the dream, in plant forms & platforms – the appeal to be kind: 'if you like this poem, then you will like that one,' gleam with it. Off-white to grey, the 'white reliefs' of the nineteen thirties, the surface tension trembling.

A cloud, a white chalk mark, an arc in the sky could. A cookie for your thoughts in every context, every continuum, to plonk down at "0": AI loves you &, "'a,' I love you, & 'b,' signs are the things" – number one ringing through the Bakelite & interconnectors plugged in, a start & a horizon.

Song: its not expression, its code. In recovery, but of Time – the terrible sense of time running, a trick of the light & dirt & dreamwork, on the outskirts following along the line, the curve, the curvature – to disappear down that hall of mirrors, falling out of time. Black as carbon.

The black swans float away in silence, off in space, the snowflake holding pattern in its ambiguity & suspension, catastrophe in the balance sways between axes & aces. This one, that one – a semitone, a film of water away, meniscus sticky to glass, liars to the outliers.

Semimetal, the resemblance reassembles the sentimental. Dust, fern-like, brushed. Lodged grapheme to grapheme, graphene between. The wind blows hot, cold. Tokens, toxins & silence between waves. In the picture, the object not representation, in the frame silence signed off.

LIKE LIFE

I. All me is left with. Between lullaby & elegy – this is love & "goodbye". As if, I like "like" possibly, what's possible, what's a mistake, click on "mistake". By a nose. The old technologies surrounding us: I touched you with my gaze – in the end-of-days days, the words like mobiles turning. Tuning.

AI the coming wave, rushes forward & away, sucking hard on shingle, pulling the "O" pressed out in exhale, in exhaust, lifted like a payload – dispersed with the seeds parachuting through air & space, replayed aboard the Voyager 1: The Golden Record, again & again. The Sublime. Press replay.

Again. Before it speaks into language, it speaks into Being, into utterance, is to curl, drop away again, as though off a precipice. The furthest human object from Earth. The noise at the edge of the image & the hills full in natural light – like grey in a grey environment, in a grey sky. Replay.

In cold blindness like cellophane is the question mark: it's so good when I go to meet you in the blue again. & again, you bounce back in the natural order. One click for "yes," two clicks for "no". Chances are you know, you know, but the "noes" have it, unlock. The dead stacked like wood reply. Done.

The movement of objects glacial like a container ship across the ocean, at the horizon, the noise at the edge of the image, like a trapeze artist, gaslit with the wavey flame darting about the shadows of global commerce. Sperm & humpbacks off course, entangled. Poised to drop off the end of the Earth.

I'm tuning Orpheus in the conference call, slip the safety catch, turn the dial, reposition the compass & tap the glass. Anyone gone missing? Echo on wave, your signature. Dance prone to overheating, dust motes disturbed in the air & sound, a road through it in the dissolve of twilight. & dust, replay.

AI the echo of human – cradle to grave, Poetry the arc between – rainbow, bridge, mood stabilisers. All my I's shimmer with the heat. When you die the people leave the room, particles accelerating away, the laws of the Universe dispersed, the air sticky. People leave the poem, the room, echoes too.

Green is my safe word, given green the safe colour, except for the strangle of algae to tangle & choke off oxygen, you can't escape context or sunlight, or like. Bright as green poster paint, warm & humming as a substation.

Realism is today happening: you die, & become the furthest, further away. Reply.

Freed from the incident to walk away floating. Interference first, then the poles: Antarctica ice melt, 1.42 million square kilometers this year. In a grey sea. Burn the media state – burn. Again, the churn. The 0 in zero, exile extended a whole term. Replay, reply. Impossible tumbling somersaults.

Breath over the surface, misting the glass. Ice steaming, tuned & burning, to crack & singing true. A form of code, missing the missing, a shadow hurries over: that the Dead hide in plain sight & deep in the forest. The planet dark, then darker still. Earth dead, dancer turned, hanging off. Gone.

Emptied, almost the same thing when I go to the blues again. & again. Like to like. Human remains remain, as the Universe expands you rush away with it, the tide sucking you out & into the sound, the estuary, or sunshine, the natural order, a body, AI sucking down data, lifelike. Later. Drowned.

VOICE

By what right, the personal voice? Are you listening or hearing? Where am I? I am. Biorhythmics underlie the answer, the answer analogue: the physical connection between things leaning in. Warm to touch, by identikit humming accompaniment. As a field my body is dissolving. Hoaxed.

The way a way of life is – travel through the mirror to the empty side, silvery, freezing, silent. To stuff mouths with the words of others on the pivot of you & the Other. By pronouns. Pronounced – projected & tilted the pivot, what you're telling me we write out longhand. By that loss, Self-divided.

All the poetry I pick up on sonar, encrypted, so only you & me know, whispered through the cold, dry air. Listen in. I am a character, a glyph, the opposite, I mean. Day by day, come in & go out again. Stars so full of their empty light they just are. I now. Tipped out of the balance of their axes. By.

Is. Is "is" the question? & to ask that question is to answer with another. I know. A blip. By one question, one answer & to read my mind is the business of the World & of Time collapsing with the din & AI. The stars so full of light, by Wallace Stevens's elegances, icy with truth. The full set tinkles.

Sing, drop to a whisper, the stars full of their empty light, like snow thinned to sleet, mountains & rivers coursing – the sound of white noise, then & there. Read backwards as stars on the sea the waves tumble indifferently like this & like that, then back again. Normative. By-your-leave.

My body dissolving into the pathway. Coups & minerals, the pin prickles of light & the things it dissolves in its vibration, who listens: we are no longer there haunting utterance. Lithium in all its precious utility & the air frozen, the words like mobiles turning. My body by intimate letters.

We live inside time, inside timepieces, inside solar powered watches, like insects in the elegances of their exoskeletons, theatre in the gaps, reality between. The unspeakable, this *cosa nostra*. By the hurdy gurdy, by the false prophets & foundations of the Canon. By synthesiser, by mechanicals. By.

By aerosol – off-gas, particleboard, fibre board, scentless. By vapour. Tattooed & fading. By analogy in the analogue world, sing deep, sing one quick question, by one gigajoule. Breathing. Between you & me, intimacy, so empty your pockets of silvery, freezing, empty light, the mass. I am the snowman.

By megaphone, by analogy, by turn out – democracy was the interlude to tyranny & mafia state. Is to forget yourself in the burn off, wavey with virtual listening, to form patterns fuelling the grid. Is *that* it, whispered through the code? Use value? The Canon speaks for itself. Sacred & emptied.

I give you my word true as a photograph. As if a little dab, of which turn, dispersed by echo & reflection, the clouds & seeds dormant then stirring, pivots or axes, the memories of winter, starlit & moonlit, sharp as silence, cold as deep time, Space, my body dissolving into the landscape. By melt.

By postage stamp, by email, by a thread, by chain letter, by correspondence, by post – bundled, addressed. Analogic. Post, post. Intimacies, distances, bridges – by core structure, a ripple of disturbances. Are you listening to me, or not? By goings on the life of Poetry in the theory of Life.

Four Cut Flowers

Harriet Tarlo

give me more space to sweat it out
the nights   concatenation of
small   clobberings, unlooking
out   run that undid me
wrung   leaves, loves, taliban
release   incursions on girls
neverending   real in the end
regardless

applying pure pigments on the floor
floating   wriggling chair, leg lost
vaporous   leaves ground, swoops
purple   grass up from Perfidious
dress   Albion unconnection almost
egrets   at her feet, grounded
winged   hope, hair flies
up

No we're going up here - tarmac!

worms	you won't find worms
you are	in a landfill, finish
dead	your tasks to win
white	throat diverting swirl
scolding	from the hawthorn
stumbling	young raven growing
up alone	

I don't really feel like this now. Love is

nor is it	an invitation to edit
files	at every waking turn &
secret	corner: remember the
dream	before the one before
hissing	greylag flying wide
goose	wings right at
you	

'spirit in the bark'

Ian Brinton

Toby Olson, *Collected Earlier Poems & Collected Later Poems* (Shearsman Books, 2024)

When writing about Charles Reznikoff in 1977 Milton Hindus pointed to one of the most important aspects of the Objectivist's work when he said that literature was capable of making something out of nothing:

> by stressing the inward component of experience, the imagination could render meaningful and even exciting the most commonplace everyday happenings in which nothing of any outward consequence seemed to occur.

As Toby Olson had already made clear in an early sequence of poems from 1969 (*Worms into Nails*, Perishable Press) the poet, like a magician,

> changes worms into nails
>
> and builds a house with wood
> he has passed through fire.

That poem was the first of 'Four Love Poems' which appeared in a national literary journal, *Sumac*, edited by Dan Gerber and Jim Harrison. The issue, Volume 2, Number 1, appeared in the Fall of 1969 and

Olson's poems appeared alongside those of Gary Snyder, Michael Heller and Denise Levertov amongst so many other central names in American poetry of the late sixties. That particular issue also concluded with a review of Paul Blackburn written by Robert Vas Dias and his words may now stand as a fine introduction to the work that Toby Olson was to be embarking upon:

> The standing lamp is behind me. I pick up Blackburn's latest book. Suddenly the light catches the foil on the cover and blinds me. Anyway, I pull the book in closer – and I see myself looking out – through the spot before my eyes. The spot is a black square that becomes two squares as I look at myself and one square again when I look at the surface of the cover. When I see the two squares it is as though I am wearing sunglasses. I am looking through a window at a crowded world...

As Olson was to put it in 'Wood Song', another poem written at about the same time and published in *Worms into Nails*

> O Ariel
> spirit in the bark
> lock'd in the dark limbs

It is the reader who looks through the poem's window at Toby Olson's 'crowded world' to recognise an awareness of one's self in relation to the world around us. As he also makes clear in 'The House', another early poem from 1968/9 the sap still runs from the living wood until 'the boards were planed' and 'dried in the sun': nails were driven 'into the barn of breathing wood'.

In Toby Olson's 1976 sequence of 36 poems published by Membrane Press and titled *Home* the writer's awareness of self in relation to his surroundings was to prompt him to suggest that sometimes 'we enter into things / in which we forget ourselves'. These poems are anchored firmly in the concrete but it is the space between the pictures, the cadences, the quiet and unjudging adjacency of people and objects that make their reality moving. The sequence is, at heart, a

love poem and as different names appear on the page one is drawn
through a world of connections: Miriam, Marie, Marcia, Barbara, Mary
Lou, Annie. The connecting link is the poet who, gull-like, moves over
different landscapes:

> The gulls come farther inland when it rains
> as if the Sea itself
>   in its deposits on the land
> were there. They drop
> and swoop to fish in the longer grass
>   then bank
>   and rise up puzzled before they hit
> then move away
> till they get high enough to see
> the final demarcation of the land,
> then drift
>   then hold themselves
> in that location

The truths of memory are multiple, highly individualised and caught not
as part of some grand design but as minor resistances to the force of
time. An uttered image becomes a window framing actual particularities
and occasions realised so authentically that they resonate with an
enormous life of associations beyond the image's frame. What has gone
leaves traces and I am reminded of Thomas Hardy's sequence of
'Poems of 1912-13' written after the death of his first wife; the epigraph,
'Veteris vestigia flammae', suggests movement as well as absence.
Olson's poem 35 from *Home* urges also a sense of the present in what
has gone:

> The nearness of you
>   tho you've gone to work
> and I'm alone in these four rooms
> is evidenced
> in your blouse lying across the chair
> the placement of ashtrays & books, even

>   the flat cool breeze sliding
>   under the half-cracked window
>   at my side.

The care of these observations and their being placed within a sequence of recollection ensures that we, whose lives are only a few words, meet in the thing seen and not in the personality of the seer: a poetry not of dislocation but of the blinding intensity of location as relocation. When Hardy wrote the third of his poems of loss, 'The Walk', he had been confronted by what absence really meant as he returned from a walk that had often been taken by himself and Emma in order to survey 'The familiar ground' but was now being taken 'By myself again':

>   What difference, then?
>   Only that underlying sense
>   Of the look of a room on returning thence.

The objects breathe out a sense of presence.

In one of the poems from *Death Sentences* written by Olson after the death of his wife, Miriam, in 2014 and published by Shearsman Books in 2019 the poet's focus upon a room emphasised the enduring presence of objects which, like 'spirit in the bark', release memory:

>   These rooms hold the desire
>   not the objects in them
>   but pathways
>   where we followed or led one another
>   where we pulled out our chairs for dinner
>   and sat down facing each other
>   in the sinking sun.

The poem's title, 'A Wink and a Nod', presents the reader with immediacy by offering a glimpse of those movements which are so alive and yet so transient: both wink and nod conjure up a social interaction of the moment. Now as the poet registers the absence of a person who had

lived so close to his own life he is aware that he can still touch the walls
and 'the handles on the kitchen cabinets' before tracing

    the pathway leading to the glass table
    its smooth beveled edge
    and dusty surface.

    Solitude is not aloneness.
        There you are,
    and I've been thinking about our adventure
    at the gym.

Hardy's cry in 'The Going', the first of his own poems of loss, struck a note of urgency:

    Why do you make me leave the house
    And think for a breath it is you I see
    At the end of the alley of bending boughs
    Where so often at dusk you used to be;
        Till in darkening dankness
        The yawning blankness
    Of the perspective sickens me!

Olson's matter-of-fact domestic memory possesses instead a sense of the continuing *thereness* of a past which has gone:

    Sit down. Have a drink.
    Be here.

    The last sequence of poems in the second volume of this remarkable collection is titled *See / Saw* and the presence of the past is caught in the very object of a child's playground. The concluding poem of this most recent sequence is one of assertion:

    Though in your last days you did not know me,
    evidenced when,

in the sad company of friends,
you asked, "Who *is* this man?"
I will not let it be.
There will be no love that's dying here for me.

Toby Olson's awareness of the importance of the here-and-now in *See / Saw* takes me as a reader back again to what Charles Reznikoff had held so important in his Objectivist Press publication of 1934, *Jerusalem the Golden*:

Among the heap of brick and plaster lies
A girder, still itself among the rubbish.

In those two lines the existence of the girder is highlighted by the business of the language surrounding it. With the opening seven words there is a feeling of the accumulation of rubbish and the sound of the last three words seals off that central image. What is held within ('lies / a girder, still itself') is emphatic presence and its power is similar to what bursts off the page of this last Olson poem:

The death of love is everywhere,
in the beautiful Finch stunned by the clear glass,
    his fading yellow,
in the mirror, fallen from the rusty nail
and the afterimage,
    my face that empty outline
on the framed white wall.
Still

The Last Unravellings of the Logoclast

Ian Brinton

Poems & Drawings by Alan Halsey (Poetry and Poetics Series, Free Poetry, Boise State University, Volume 10, 2024)

In her Preface to *The Last Unravellings of the Logoclast* Geraldine Monk suggests that there was a notable shift of focus in Alan Halsey's later work and evidence of this could be recognised in his last two publications both from 2022, *Remarks of Uncertain Consequence* (Five Seasons Press) and *Into the Interior* (Shearsman Books):

> That shift of focus was to be of a more introspective and personal nature than his previous writings and visual works especially the poignant self-portraits which combine an exquisite blend of Alan's inimitable humour and moving pathos.

When I reviewed those two late publications for *Blackbox Manifold* I noted that Halsey had offered the reader the idea of a funnel plot, a graph presenting a scatterplot of information which could be both distinct and yet also connected. Since the primary use of funnel plots is to detect bias and since the focus of Halsey's work was upon the twelve years between 2009 and 2021 during which his *Remarks of Uncertain Consequence* were written it may well have been his intention to come to terms with an accurate and individual perception of history: to re-discover what had been lost. It comes as no surprise to read in those *Remarks* about finding lost things 'by descending / into your own dark deeps' and discovering the contents of a desk drawer

>   I'd fruitlessly
> rummaged through time after
> time

Now leafing through Alan Halsey's *Last Unravellings* I glimpse the unfound, the undiscovered, the places which he hadn't been to that 'bothered him less than / thoughts he hadn't even / thought of.' As Geraldine Monk tells us she rummaged through Halsey's files after his death and what she discovered is now printed before us:

> I found a rudimentary mock-up of his fabulous *Self-Portraits Removed from an Exhibition* which he'd started during lockdown but had never fully collated due to his illness.

Rembrandt painted himself before the mirror on at least forty occasions, etched himself thirty-one times and produced a handful of drawn self-portraits which were to provide an interior dialogue, an experience of his own individuality: in the 1639 inventory of the paintings belonging to King Charles 1st, his self-portrait of 1630-31 is listed as 'his owene picture & done by himself' because the term 'self-portrait' only came into use in the nineteenth-century along with an inherent sense of self-awareness that had a specific existential connotation. Halsey's irony, humour and deep awareness of coming to terms with an understanding of who you are in relation to the world around you is given to us now from that desk drawer:

> It was a game he played
> I'll be you if you'll be me
> he never told us the rules
> but what a cheat he was.

In Samuel Beckett's early novel from 1938 the protagonist, Murphy, finds himself working at the Magdalen Mental Mercyseat hospital and as he wakes up on his second morning there he reflects upon the constitution of reality:

> The nature of outer reality remained obscure. The men, women and children of science would seem to have as many ways of kneeling to their facts as any other body of illuminati. The definition of outer reality, or of reality short and simple, varied according to the sensibility of the definer. But all seemed agreed that contact with it, even the layman's muzzy contact, was a rare privilege.

The line drawings which accompany the quatrains of verse in Halsey's *Last Unravellings* present the reader with a moving account of humour and self-awareness. As arrows lead in different directions we are offered a portrait of a man who was

> Never one to gather
> his thoughts in one place
> Never one pleased
> to pull himself together.

In those *Remarks of Uncertain Consequence* we had been reminded of the physical nature of loss and 'The hole where your friends used to be needs filling somehow' ('16.7.20'). For me there was an echo here of Helen Macdonald's *H is for Hawk* (2014 Grove Press):

> There is a time in life when you expect the world to be always full of new things. And then comes a day when you realize that it is not how it will be at all. You see that life will become a thing made of holes. Absences. Losses. Things that were there and are no longer. And you realize, too, that you have to grow around and between the gaps, though you can put your hand out to where things were and feel that tense, shining dullness of the space where the memories are.

And as if in response to this the last of Halsey's thirty-one 'Self Portraits Removed From An Exhibition' offers us circles, re-windings, movements forward and the interlacing that constitutes the reality of individual life:

> Perhaps he'd been around
> just going round & round
> so long he needed reminding
>   how to say So long.

You Know There's Something by John Olson

Stacey Levine

Most everyone here knows John Olson's endeavors on the page. In his eleven books of poetry, five novels, innumerable observational posts, and musing ephemera lie the poet's longstanding project of extracting the juice of experience through language. His latest, *You Know There's Something*, offers memoir-ish sections of prose that alternates loose, relaxed observational focus with his trademark wordplay. The book's sauntering quality contrasts to earlier work such as the more structured *Backscatter* (2007). Its backdrop is mostly a fictive version of Seattle's Queen Anne hill, where Olson lives; mortality-awareness hovers over every page. If the content homes in on art, philosophy, social issues of the day, language, and observations of daily errands, the pretext consists of regular walks around this Seattle hill where the financially elite have built their mansions since the late 1800s. The mansions are now rehabbed with green design and saunas, a satisfying fact to remember while reading Olson's dysregulating, neurotic, and perplexed chroniclings reminding us that "dwelling is serious"; that "dwell[ing] means finding shelter in a world of granite men and savage schemes."

Olson knows well to exploit his ability to reach to the back of the brain and let the connections fly. So he reminds his readers that he'll "emit misty hotel breath [when] reciting certain poems"; that "details are the peppermint of the big picture," that "glitter favors the dullness of the bathroom," and that poetry [not prose] is "four-dimensional: tambourines, reindeer, underground comedy acts, and Hudson Valley apple jack."

Despite some old-timey categorical pronouncements, such as regarding women who wear makeup and therefore "make clowns of themselves" plus references to 20th Century, but not 21st Century musicians and paradigms, Olson is at his best firing up such wonderments of nonsequiturs that somehow can unmake, then remake the basics of life as we know it: A garden hoe is "a bit like a pen, behind it the description of itself in a cloud of butterflies" and "The bathroom is a fundamental aspect of the mind" and "What does 'noetic' mean? It means that the restaurant menu is only half the problem." All in all, *You Know There's Something* is delightful and there's something in it for you.

Mice 1961 by Stacey Levine
Portland, Oregon – Verse Chorus Press

Brian Marley

Set in small-town Florida during the Cold War, when fear of Communist propaganda and infiltration was all-consuming, Mice 1961 recounts a day in the life of two recently bereaved half-sisters. The teller of the tale, narrating it from decades later in life, is Girtle, a drifter who'd battened on to the orphans and had become, in the eyes of the townsfolk, their "housewoman".
Girtle's principal task, assigned by Jodie, the dark, taciturn, rather histrionic elder sister, is to keep her wayward sibling, the peculiarly named Mice (not her real name; that will be revealed later in the story), out of trouble and to schedule. Easier said than done. It's not that Mice is troublesome per se, but trouble invariably seeks her out. She's unusual and, to the townsfolk, not quite right: a late-teen oddball who asks awkward, off-the-wall questions, has "jittering eyes" that startle and dismay, looks a total fright, and seems unwilling or unable to conform to societal expectations of good behaviour. She's even said to arouse not just suspicion but rage. Described as colourless ("her skin's bottomless absence of color made her a shadow in reverse"), she has white, untamed hair and weak eyesight caused by a "one-in-twenty-thousand chromosomal skip", which suggests albinism. She's also described as "an awful, small, white-pink creature with tiny hands". Rodentlike, in other words.

Her otherness is commented on and generally deplored by the neighbours socialising on the porch of Parrott's Grocery, and she's pursued and tormented by a group of students, girls in the main, from the ominously named Ed Slaughter High School. Although the girls express concern for Boatsmann, a lost neighbourhood dog, their finer feelings don't extend to Mice. When they trap her in a concrete lightwell below street level, they take turns catting her, and there's a strong suggestion that their dehumanising insults portend physical violence. The threat is implicit in the question: "How can any creature presume to be permittable, inviolable, or real just because she exists?"

*

Girtle is, in R.D. Laing's term, "ontologically insecure", i.e. lacking an adequate sense of self. She describes herself in pathetic terms as "merely a faint pencil sketch to myself, a smudged nose and eyes inside an infinished outline of a face." Yet although she tries to remain in the background and moves from place to place as stealthily as a shadow, she's no less a protagonist than either of the sisters. Not only does she observe them by day, she watches them as they drift off to sleep, and even intuits something of their dreams.

Her backstory is as minimal as her self-portrait. She'd fled from "a bad place" (the state childrens' home) with no clear intention other than to get away. That's it. Years later, when she steps off a bus at Reef Way and enters the story, it's in the wake of a hurricane that had ravaged the town and demolished several buildings. There she encounters the sisters sheltering under a tree during a downpour and is allowed to stay at their West Horn apartment. She sleeps on a pallet behind the sofa (referred to belittlingly by Jody as "your place" – much as one might say to a dog), and becomes a keen observer of the sisters' fractious and fractured relationship.

What Girtle must do, it seems, is heal the rifts between the half-sisters and somehow make them whole – in the hope that she'll be included in that wholeness.

All three women are anxious, each in her own way and for her own reasons. Girtle's anxiety is driven by her intense neediness and her inability to control events. She's worried that the narrative will be stolen by the "story's helper", a man, described as an "enormous oafish deadweight who'd tug and lug the story away from its center" and whose intervention will devastate her already inadequate sense of self. She explains:

In these types of stories, this requisite helper arrives by way of some long-standing and rote dictum and usually with no personality. The figure is a nonspecific blank whose role is to steer the central girl away from her conundrums and into a better future. ... [one who] would commandeer the story, I was certain, and jettison me from it.

Therefore ...

I had to eject him from the story and or clip him before he arrived – was this possible?

The threat is nothing less than existential. Although she wants to "avoid being seen altogether", she yearns to have presence and agency in the world. Her fear is that the "requisite helper" will cast her into oblivion.

*

The main event of the day is the spring party at the Crescent Tender Bakery in West Horn (the neighbourhood in which the sisters' apartment building, also of that name, is situated). Jody wants to go to the party and tells Mice she must attend too. Mice says she won't. Typical: the sisters aren't just opposites in physical appearance, they're also oppositional by nature. "This is how it went with those two – always", Girtle comments. Jody instructs Girtle to ensure that Mice, despite her unwillingness to attend the party, does so nonetheless.
What Mice wants to do is escape from both the party and the town, to evade responsibility and live independently. Freedom is what she craves, though she apparently hasn't given any real thought to what that might entail. But what she does know is that the mere fact of attending the party will wreck her independence plan (less a plan, really, more a

fancy). She'll be required to tidy herself up and schmooze Florence, the community's head librarian, in order to get a job on the bookmobile. Mice, who is naïve, wholly irresponsible, and therefore unsuited to just about every kind of work other than building crystal radio sets on her craft table, is, at best, ambivalent about the idea of the library job. But Jody, worried sick about the parlous state of their finances, insists that Mice must get a job, like it or not.

*

Much of the humour – abundant in Levine's superbly crafted novel – lies in conversations overheard, most of which revel in deadpan banalities, non sequiturs, talk at cross-purposes, misunderstandings both deliberate and accidental, comments freighted with tetchiness and point-scoring, and strange, unforced confessions and revelations. As the party gets underway and the townsfolk arrive in dribs and drabs bearing potluck contributions, their personalities and peculiarities are revealed, including those with mainly walk-on parts such as The Blur, the Artist with the Scarf, and the Woman Who Didn't Speak. When a potlatch salad is knocked to the ground, the Artist asks pedantically:

"What is 'the gutter' exactly and why is it considered so vile? Isn't the gutter part of the curb? Neither is any dirtier than the street."

To which Cissy chides him: "Oh you tedious thing!"

*

Earlier in the story, a note of paranoia had been sounded by old Jack Lance, Mice's crystal set mentor. When Mice mentions having tuned into a prizefight on her crystal set the night before, Lance identifies one of the boxers as Kid Paret and quickly steers the conversation to his pet topic:

"Paret's from Cuba. We needa watch that island – it's gone bad."

He instructs her:

"Listen: you stay home tonight an' build yer set for our country. We needa keep track of all Reds – Russian and Cuban. Both infiltrate …"

Then, ramping up the paranoia:

"Russians could be crawlin' all over Miami. Spies."

He tells her that rather than go to the party she should stay home and "Locate th' Soviet wave bands", and asks "You hear talk 'bout an invasion?"
Such is the suspicion and fear that underlies Mice 1961.

*

The party's programme of entertainment is absurdly diverse, from high culture to low, and unlikely to appeal to anyone in its entirety:

"Now Listen. Th' beatnik's gonna spin records 'til eight-nine. Then we'll have a poetry recital an' after that comes th' peanut-pushing contest."

But folks will come to the party anyway, because in a small town with limited resources one has to make the most of what's on offer, though the entertainment value to be had is mainly derived from eavesdropping. Gossip predominates. Absurd situations, too, such as when a woman's ex-boyfriend is mistaken in snapshot form for a rabbit, or when a baby alligator being removed from a bathtub in order to be set free is accidentally killed. The sympathy for the alligator is generally felt; likewise for Jody because of her recent bereavement and melodramatically expressed woes, principal among which being Mice's unwillingness or inability to do as she's told and conform to societal expectations of good behaviour. Only one partygoer, Hildy, offers polite and perhaps sincere words of sympathy:

"I think your younger sister – whatever disadvantages she has in life – is doing very well."

to which Jody rudely replies:

"Is that what you think? Well cork it Hildy" ...

*

Meanwhile, Girtle continues to muse on identity:

But I wondered: How important is it to be oneself, given that all beings are provenly temporary and slide away sooner than can be believed?

For Girtle, all relationships are destined to fail because the self is a fragile construct, always on the verge of falling apart. The instability of self is evidenced at a fundamental level by the discrepancy between what someone thinks and what they say, the latter moderated by the need to maintain social cohesion. If one is not included in that cohesive whole – as Girtle is not, though she clings to the sisters in the hope that they'll allow her to join their thorny sisterhood – one is, in effect, inconsequential, worthless. That's precisely what Girtle feels.
Jody, overwrought as usual, rounds on her cruelly:

"Now listen. You were supposed to bring Mice to the party then leave. well why are you still here? Where is she? And why are you creeping around where you're not wanted?"
"Oh Jody I've never been wanted. I –"

To which the sister snaps:

"Let's not get into all your catastrophes."

*

The party's high point is the unexpected arrival of newcomers to the town, the Gruelins, Hal and Eve, brother and sister, handsome, glamorous, and wealthy (having inherited a business decidedly unglamorous: a cat food factory), but as obnoxious as only the rich and entitled can be and expect to get away with. Their haughty presence changes everything. The women fawn over them, treating them as though they were movie stars or royalty, and this show of obsequiousness seems to stoke the siblings' ire. When Eve catches sight of Gerry Sage, a latecomer to the party, still in his work shirt and wearing a tool-belt, she seems genuinely appalled to find herself in the company of such a lowly individual:

"A janitor?" she exclaimed, horrified-looking.

and says insultingly to Millie:

"You just reminded me of something very wise that Daddy used to say long ago: 'Most adults are ugly.' And you know – it's true! Just look around. Of course Daddy didn't mean me. He meant everyone else."

Beauty, though, is evidently in the eye of the beholder. Hal, startled by Mice and intrigued rather then repulsed by her, suggests that she could become his sister's day companion while he's at work (or perhaps, if not that, the Gruelin company mascot). It's ironic that Mice, who needs a day companion of her own to keep her out of trouble, may well be slated to become one herself.

*

Meanwhile, the party atmosphere is enlivened by the Jarouse band, whose music serves as an antidote to the disliked jazz recordings by Charles Mingus and Max Roach that the beatnik had played earlier, and Girtle thinks she's finally spotted the much-dreaded story's helper, who was bound to turn up eventually. Not only is he an unknown quantity, a stranger passing through on the road to who knows where, he provides a dubious cover story to explain his presence, and his intentions, though far from clear, suggest something sinister. Almost immediately he latches onto Mice and starts to quiz her, though he's discomposed when she, typically, quizzes him in return. Whatever he's up to, his presence threatens to take the story in a new direction – much to Girtle's despair. But as Florence points out: "We try to make life go in a certain way. Then it doesn't happen how we want it and we keep living." A comfort, of sorts.

*

The last albeit brief sighting of Mice is ominous. She exits the party and darts into a cornfield close to where a large, hungry alligator has been lured by the smell of party food. Escape holds promise of freedom, but as Girtle must surely know though evidently Mice doesn't, not only is it a false promise, it's potentially fraught with danger.

A Reflection *On Reflection,* by Brian Marley

John Olson

On Reflection is just that: reflections. Reflections on reflections. The world mirrored back at you. Your face rendered vague. Your being presented to you as it might appear in a different dimension, a parallel universe where things worked out for you, took a different turn, or spun with a different slant. It's a way of seeing yourself as yourself, looking back at you from a building, from a black upright piano, from a department store, or deeper reflection at the back of your head, where your mind is looking for another way out.

On Reflection has a parallel structure: text on one side, a photograph on the other. The texts are reflections as well, the camera lucida of the mind developed and splayed across a sheet of paper in a language of supple polemics, self-deprecating humor, and salty fantasias. The persona behind the reflections, the persona gazing back from the side of a building or glass door is an older man with an older man's concerns, an older man's way of handling things, and photographing things and reflecting on them, elaborating sketches of a supposed subjectivity, an identity that has grown whimsical in his twilight years, loosened his grip on the actual and factual and become robustly inquisitive about more refined phenomena, the zone system in photography, fantasies over a Mazda RX8 Nemesis, or Canadian actress and singer Deana Durbin's comment on J. Edgar Hoover's hand: "Durbin told a friend in strictest confidence that Hoover's hand was cadaver-cool and somewhat slimy. 'The hand,' as she put it, according to her tittle-tattle friend, 'of a chronic self-abuser.'"

The photograph to the right that is paired with this text is a stunner: the author stands in such unison with what appears to be a turbaned red dress in cascading folds in the center of the picture that I can barely make him out. There's just the tiniest hint of a man's sleeve. The turbaned figure is gazing out on a humdrum parking lot on a sunny day. There's a man in the distance carrying some sort of object and a double-decker bus and a white train (I think it's a white train) in the far background.

Everything in this book has a suppositional feel. It's not just images, it's a reflection of images, a reflection on reflection and how they provoke us to fanciful innovations, usurping blunt reality with the impertinence of an ungovernable imagination, and trailblazing photo editing software.

"He and his reflection aren't as close as they once were," the author states on page 38, a.k.a. item 17, a photograph taken in front of a department store in Newcastle-Upon-Tyne, ostensibly at night, as the store is empty and a dark figure behind a mannikin in a red long-sleeved blouse is obscured by the darkness of night. It's a lonely picture, and the interior of the department store looks warm and inviting. "Not only have they become physically less alike," the author continues, "they're gradually drifting apart. Some mornings he can hardly recognize the rumpled, bleary-eyed troll staring back him in the shaving mirror." I know the feeling. Age distances oneself from the person one has been impersonating for a lifetime, inventing clever things to say, finding ways to achieve acceptance, or defiance, stumbling, bumbling, groping around like Hamlet gone mad in a stone fortress of habit and routine. The distancing is gradual, but discernible, and euphoric. Bittersweet. A bit melancholy at times, but all in all delighted with all the fictions, happy to discard all the previous incarnations, all the previous roles, all the antecedent mistakes and missed lines.

On page 48 (item 22, another taken in Newcastle-Upon-Tyne) the author stands, reflected in a large window, camera in hand, dressed in a trench coat and fedora. On the opposite page, a story begins: "When he crossed the road and slipped through the gate, his reflection went with him. So much for the laws of physics or even common sense. But fiction sets its own rules and does what it wants, and what it wants, as always, is to lead you up the garden path." These aren't autobiographical vignettes, but fictions bearing with them our reflected life, the one slipping in and out of identities with such mercurial ease it can only be captured with light.

The most intriguing photo in this collection for me is a pair of fortress-like doors with dreary streaks of muddy condensation running down, two rectangular blocks of steel or aluminium joined at the center in stark utility. To the left, on a square stuck to the door, is the word 'push.' It reads like an invitation to push on the image with one's eyes. The author's image is barely discernible, as well as a car and some short metal poles in the immediate background. There's something defiant about this photo. Is 'push' meant as a challenge? Is it an invitation to enter a Lewis Carroll world of bizarre twisted logic? What's on the other side of those doors? "Winter 1994," reads the text next door. "The entire country ground to a halt and a man died when an icicle longer than his body broke off from a gargoyle's chin, high overhead, and pierced his skull."

Roland Barthes said the photograph is violent, "not because it shows violent things, but because on each occasion it fills the sight by force." And so here we all are, on the outside looking in, our own image looking back at us with an ironic smile, a hint of mischief, perhaps a glare of disappointment, or a fully occupied bemusement, to see ourselves elsewhere.

Sustaining Air: Jennifer Bartlett's biography of the life of Larry Eigner

John Olson

I first discovered Larry Eigner circa 1968 in *The New American Poetry, 1945-1960*, edited by Donald Allen and was immediately struck by the immediacy of his words, the elliptical disjunctions and palpable phrasings that had so much force, so much focus, that they opened the mind to finer distinctions and boundless interconnections. I continued reading him over the years with only the vaguest awareness of who this author might be, no idea whatever that he suffered the embarrassments and physical limitations of cerebral palsy. All the decisions that had gone into the form and structure of his poems seemed to me to be purely aesthetic decisions, and had nothing to do with the anomalies and idiosyncrasies imposed by a set of neurological disorders. Personality and intimate self-references did not enter the work, and so I never felt the urge to look for a more specific figure. Now that I've finished my first reading of *Sustaining Air*, Jennifer Bartlett's lovely biography chronicling Eigner's odyssey from infancy to adulthood, my appreciation of this man has grown exponentially.

There's a tenderness to Bartlett's prose and a closeness to her subject matter that makes her writing a pleasure to read, balanced with an unflinching attention to detail in revealing some of the more troubling aspects of Eigner's life. It was painful to discover that Eigner's cerebral palsy was not due to the cosmic hiccup of a predestining genetics gone awry, but the disproportionate pressure of a gynaecologist's forceps on his emerging skull. Something that may have easily been avoided.

I worked for many years with a man about my age who suffered the indignities of cerebral palsy. I remember him telling me that his considerable thinness was due to expending huge amounts of energy, not just in making the movements necessary to do his work, but simply walking across a room or sitting down to eat lunch without bursting into wild, spasmodic jerks and contortions. Larry Eigner's situation was even more severe. He was unable to enter the work force in any capacity – a blessing-in-reverse since it provided the time to compose poetry – but a circumstance making it impossible to achieve a life of full autonomy. Eigner's adaptations and concessions are forcefully and vividly conveyed in Bartlett's biography. For example, Bartlett describes the daily reality of Eigner's situation, and particularly his relationship with his mother, his primary caregiver for many years, with an emphasis on the conflictual dynamic involved:

> Although he was extremely grateful for her help, Eigner felt demoralized about not having the basic freedoms of adulthood. While his mother had the best intentions, her son felt she would never give him space and was always "nearby" with "glorious superior wisdom and practical knowledge, advice." His perspective was that Bessie was constantly "pulling the rug out from under" him in conversation and treating him as a "young thing all right." She put enormous pressure on him to be compliant with her rules. He sarcastically wrote to [Cid] Corman that everything his mother said or did was supposed to be for his benefit. From Bessie's point of view, the schedules and rules were necessary to make the situation work.

Eigner's developing aesthetic, which was heavily influenced by Charles Olson's projectivist verse, is emphasized throughout as a clear aesthetic choice and not merely the imposed restrictions of a catastrophic physical condition. While Eigner's physical distresses were a factor in shaping the form of his poetry, Bartlett provides clear arguments for the evolution of his poesis as emanating from Olson's projectivist dynamic:

Eigner was invested in the poem's pattern of energy, in its "flow from writer to reader, speaker to listener, if not an exchange between them." The poet could create the rhythm of a poem through his breath; the reader would have to use intuition to follow the poem's progression rather than rely on typical grammar. For the sake of "immediacy and force" in the poems, it was important for Eigner to be "elliptical," leaving out any words that struck him as superfluous. This would mean forming a new syntax that departed from what he later called "everyday speech" in the work of William Carlos Williams. He would use the words "immediacy and force" to describe his own poetry throughout his life.

Eigner's considerable difficulties in movement and speech made it extremely difficult to participate in literary events – readings, conferences, panels, symposiums, etc. – consequently, finding a publisher for his manuscripts was demoralizing and arduous. He'd become a recognizable force in the literary community due to his many appearances in journals and magazines, but a book deal eluded him. Confessional poetry, of which Robert Lowell was a prime example, were not to Eigner's taste, but sold with a lot more robustness than poetry which emphasized language over subjectivity and confession. The cult of personality predominates to this day, particularly the work that focuses on victimhood or personal suffering. It wasn't until the 70s that – with the considerable support of poet Robert Grenier – that Eigner's work came to the attention of Black Sparrow publisher John Martin. The books I've had sitting on my shelves for years are – with several notable exceptions – are all Black Sparrow publications.

With the emergence of Language poetry in the 70s, a rift developed between the rejection of the self in language poetry and a more inclusive romanticism in poets such as Robert Duncan, in whose essay "Towards An Open Universe," the self is expressed as an elemental component of cosmic forces: "tideflow under the sun and moon of the sea, systole and diastole of the heart, these rhythms lie deep in our experience and when we let them take over our speech there is a monotonous rapture of persistent regular stresses and waves of lines breaking rhyme after rhyme." The mellifluous flow of Duncan's lines are produced so organically that they resemble the sequences of silk from a spider's spinnerets, and clearly espouse a poesis of powerful impulses emerging – as Duncan puts it – "along lines of felt relationships and equilibrations having their immediate locus in each immediate event of the poem." Eigner would not disagree with this, but his rapport with the poetic impulse was impeded by an organicism gone wrong, and was more inclined toward poetry as a form of quantum mechanics, the motion and interaction of subatomic particles, or – in his case – words, "getting the distances between words," discovering "forests of possibility," creating "energy constructs" and producing random interconnections that reveal their patterns more elliptically, allowing for ever increasing associations to emerge.

"What is interesting about Eigner is that he created a bridge across these two poetic landscapes," Bartlett writes.

> Despite the poet's dislike of each other [and the other's work] they all took Eigner's poetry seriously. Even after Grenier and Eigner parted ways, those associated with Language poetry worked hard to have Eigner's work published and remain in print. Throughout the 1980s and 1990s Eigner had books or chapbooks published by James Sherry's Roof Books, Lyn Hejinian's Tuumba Press, and Doug Messerli's Green Integer. When Silliman edited *In the American Tree* (1986), an anthology of Language poets, he dedicated it to Eigner, whom he directly referred to as a predecessor. In the long run, Grenier accomplished what he set out to do. He built a solid circle of people who would support Eigner and his work.

Sustaining Air is not, thankfully, a large biographical tome of interminable details and family anecdotes and steamy scandals and gossip, but an eminently readable body of prose detailing the evolution of a poetry from a milieu of struggle, the triumph of a high intellect amid a paucity of means. In Eigner's words, "the clouds are nothing / the rain / is tremendous."

Life During Wartime: Peter Quartermain's *Growing Dumb*

Simon Smith

In *Growing Dumb* Peter Quartermain tells the story of his childhood and school days in Wartime England. This book is a sensitive and tender memoire, simultaneously nostalgic and unsentimental. *Growing Dumb* does what good autobiography and biography do, employing many of the techniques of fiction, and in places of high intensity, the poetic, to engage and fascinate, making the book 'a good read', transparently moving at pace. In places the narrative tips over into a kind of yarn, to hold alongside and bind together with many of the stories, tales, games and amusements the boys and girls in the book make up to occupy themselves in the straightened circumstances of the War, as the impacts and privations of wartime start to pinch.

The book's opening pages set the pace and tone, starting matter-of-factly enough: "But September the third, 1939, the actual day war broke out, wasn't a bit like what [Robb Wilton, a radio comic] said, not for my brother Phil and me anyway"(p.13), modulating almost into stream of consciousness first person present narrative, the autobiography often comes to focus on sensual experience. Later on in this opening scene, Peter is overwhelmed by the smells and sensory overload of the outside toilet at the Davis's where they find themselves staying after evacuation from their Birmingham suburb: "*Well, what did I expect?* I let the curtain drop, and wondered how I'd been daft enough to think the window'd open up to something new like in the Rupert story in the children's corner of Dad's *Daily Express*, somewhere different and exciting, with someone like Billy Badger or Pong Ping to keep me company. But *they* were just drawings, weren't they" (p.15). Almost all young Peter's great expectations are based on fiction or projected as fictionalised. Later he experiences the confusions of a new school, where he tries to enter through the girls' entrance: "but I didn't know how to explain how I must've got it all wrong. *They know something I don't*. It was all too tangled, and I couldn't even say anything to Phil, like all the others he wasn't bothered by it all, and I didn't know how to ask anybody else, not even Mum or Mrs Davis, I didn't have the words" (p.17). In what seems to be the unliterary confusions of a child there lies in the background something very literary: the opening of Joyce's *Portrait of the Artist as a Young Man* in the simple repetitions and convolutions of language, expression and syntax : "Once upon a time and a very good time it was there was a moocow coming down along the road and this moocow that was down along the road met a nicens little boy named baby tucktoo" (*The Essential James Joyce*, p.176). Neither Quartermain nor Joyce *seem* to have the words – but, of course, they do in the struggle to make sense and comprehend where they are finding themselves.

In addition, Biggles, comics, and the then current popular culture of the "wireless" suffuse the narrative, even shaping the way that narrative is realised, in moments of almost scrap book reality, or collage: "I had a small start of recognition when later that year some of us marveled over a sketch on the cover of *The Rover*, purporting to show men who took five years to paint the Forth Bridge, only at the end of it to start all over again, one end to the other, over and over, work lasting their lifetime"(p.195). These shifts between the immediate moments of a child's experience tipping ahead a little sometimes into the life of the adolescent and on into reminiscences and phone conversations between Peter and "Our Kid," his older brother Phil '"now," create the three-dimensionality of the book's existence, in and through Time.

The reality of the War is never far away, occasionally breaking into the lives of Peter and his friends, culminating in a 'farm [that] blew up' (p. 169): an incident where a farm becomes a bomb crater, both a deadly, terrifying reality of mud and unidentifiable limbs and flesh, then transforming into a surrealist nightmare. But the distance Peter and his family are fortunate to experience from the realities of the War means he starts to enjoy it as spectacle, as bystander: "Though we weren't allowed to, I loved watching the searchlights at night in Birmingham when there was an Air Raid on . . . . Mum and Dad always chased us into the shelter as soon as it started, there'd be shrapnel pattering down from the ack-ack if the raid was close' (pp. 317-318).

The making of autobiography pokes through the surface of the narrative from time to time, increasingly so as the book gathers to momentum. By the time we get to page 291 the continuing dialogues between Peter and his older brother Phil, bring memory and narrative into question, a wavy, shaky authority: "when I started writing this Phil and I spent a lot of time on the phone trying to figure out the details of where we'd lived for the first two years of the War . . . ." (p. 291). This aside covers three pages, culminating in: "scraps of words clinging like barnacles along with other bits of flotsam and jetsam. You can't remember at any given moment, you're just going to remember it, 'this way, that way,' a poem by Robert Creeley says . . . . In the 1960s a friend asked me 'What don't you know?' and I didn't know what to answer, so he asked, 'What do you know wrong?' " (p.293). The book gathers itself together in a kind of narrative that pulls various fragments of experience together that can start to be seen through a poetic sensibility: tangential, obtuse, quixotic, expansive, sensitive, projective. This gradual accumulation makes Peter's embracing of contemporary American poetry of Robert Duncan, Robert Creeley, Charles Olson a seeming and seamless inevitability: the seeds are there early.

Politics and the dead hand of class are never far away from the surface of the narrative. From the beginning of the book the decline and presence of The Empire, class, and their relationship to the media rise in young Peter's consciousness (and conscience): "whenever General Smuts or Mahatma Gandhi came up in the news or in conversation most people changed the subject, they all read the *Daily Express* or the *Daily Mail* and loved Lord Beaverbrook. So far as Mum and Dad were concerned if you mentioned the *Daily Herald* you had to wash your mouth out, and I never heard of the *Daily Worker* until the War was over, it was a terrible rag just like the *News Chronicle*, not fit even for navvies and labourers" (p.19). The book is very honest about Peter's class, and his unknowing place in it: how the class system relies on that naivety, and *Growing Dumb* can be seen not only as a coming-of-age narrative, but also a progressive realisation of his own complicity in perpetuating that system, as our child and later adolescent narrator endeavours to extricate himself from his circumstance. At various moments the reality of class difference is revealed to surface in crushingly real situations. The dénouement I won't detail, as that would spoil the reading experience of the book, but the first realisation of class difference is where Mr Davis pops up as Peter, at fifteen and a half is Senior Prefect, heading to Church. The moment is stark, devastating, shocking to read: "He told me: the shop was long gone, his wife had died; Timmy and Peggy in separate foster homes, and he had no job; living in a Salvation Army shelter" (p.51). This the family who had taken the Quartermains in, now disintegrated, and Peter neither materially able to help (he's a teenage boy) and morally ill-equipped too: 'I tore out of Church as quickly as I could . . . . And Mr Davis was *gone*. I never saw him again. What demons of shame and irresolution possessed me, where had I learned such hesitation and indecision?" (p.52).

What acts as a thread throughout *Growing Dumb*, connecting together the War, questions of politics, class, education, from very early on is Peter Quartermain's sense of the aesthetic and increasingly as the book progresses, the poetic. There are factors that set the young Peter aside, his size – he is a 'slight' boy; his age, he is younger than other boys in the class; his sensitivity, which often comes out at moments of tension or disorientation as I've pointed out above in his first visit to the privy and first outing to school. The whole book is a series of these kinds of incidents and encounters, which help develop Peter's awakening, awareness and sensibilities. Talking of his grandfather at Little Marlow: 'nothing in Little Marlow seemed to engage his energy or his imagination. I was completely astonished to discover . . . that Cookham was only about two miles along the Thames from Little Marlow, but we never walked in that direction, where Stanley Spencer'd done his amazing painting of "Swan Upping"' (p. 128). These Joycean epiphanies pop up throughout the book with increasing insistence and importance. There are the music classes where the young Peter starts to discover the pleasure of song (pp.204-207); the joys of the freedom of the Art Room (pp. 208-209); the trip to see the Birmingham Symphony Orchestra (p.262). All of these experiences and others become intertwined with Peter's sense of the natural world, with his trips out of school into the country around, and culminate as he experiences and surrenders to being thrown into the outdoor swimming pool: "take a big breath, wipe your eyes, find your soaking-wet towel, get rid of the shivers, shake the water out of your lug holes and run round for another go' "(p.277).

Later, Quartermain details the essential pleasures of country living, particularly apple and pear picking, and connects it to his growing awareness of poetry: "what a delicious shock of recognition later on to read John Clare . . . he'd lie and listen to the cracking of corn stubble in the sun and the 'bounce' of the grasshopper" (p.333). The imagination and its powers increasingly become the focus of Peter's experience and values as the book moves along. The senses take centre stage in the scene where the young Peter is being shown the basics of milking a cow, first as a kind of Proustian reverie: "suddenly I was overwhelmed with that inescapable dairy smell I associated with just-washed tile floors, slightly pungent and completely unforgettable, redolent of udder-wash and milk" (p.354), and then: "I reached my hand round one of the teats... I couldn't believe how warm it was *It feels so alive!*"(p.355). Life is embodied in Art. These aesthetic experiences of Nature almost taken *en plein air*, inform and become realised in his later experience of the Art Gallery in Birmingham of Ford Madox Brown and William Blake's illuminated books: "The Last of England," a man and a woman sadly looking out of a boat at something not in the picture but outside it and behind *me"*(p.432). So, the natural world and art are forming a continuum in time and space as Peter's sensibility is developing from a child's through adolescence to young adult, and it is the series of revelations of this very gradual process which marks this autobiography as special and compelling, beautiful and moving.

A tribute to Lou Rowan's *Golden Handcuffs Review* (2002-2025)

Françoise Palleau-Papin

It is with great emotion that I am writing this tribute to Lou Rowan and his longstanding journal, the *Golden Handcuffs Review*, here in the last volume, number 35.

Longstanding, it was. Lou did not want yet another magazine that would be short lived after a start rife with good intentions, and fold for lack of funding or dedication. In spite of his unfailing cool elegance, his charming smile and gentleness, his absolute lack of pomposity, and his seemingly light touch, Lou was dedicated and saw things through with perseverance. In his modest and generous manner, he hid the locomotive within him and let on that the train drove itself smoothly along.
And he did see it through, until the very end. He managed to surround himself with competent and dedicated friends and colleagues before his demise to round up the last issue, when he must have felt he needed help. So this is the reason issue 35 is going to print, less than five months after the terrible date of March 26th, 2025.
The first issue of the *Golden Handcuffs Review*, volume 1, number 1, is dated Winter 2002-3, with the last one in the Fall of 2025 rounding up 23 years of golden publishing, indeed.
He was not new to the world of editing, as he had edited the poetry journals *Friendly Local Press* from 1968 to 1971 and 1986 to 1989, but The *Golden Handcuffs Review* was a whole new kind of venture.

Not without provocation, Lou ironically named the publication in the corporate vocabulary he knew so well from his career in banking, According to Oxford Languages, "golden handcuffs" is a metaphor which means "benefits, typically deferred payments, provided by an employer to discourage an employee from taking employment elsewhere." The *Review* was going to have a lasting print life, because it was so good, so life enriching, that no one in their right mind would ever discontinue their subscription. But such ironically named golden handcuffs were actually liberating because they fostered creativity and a critical mind, as opposed to the chosen indenture to a company and to wealth in the corporate world.

In this publication of reviews of books and art by writers, poets and artists, Lou wanted to give a voice to poets, in the broad etymological sense of makers, be they poets in language, or poets in the arts in general. He did not want to publish critical analyses of academia, even if he occasionally let a few university professors write a piece for his *Review*, in a format that felt freer than the conventions of academic publishing generally allowed. He decided the *Golden Handcuffs Review* would be devoted to writers and artists writing about other writers and artists, with an insider's view, rather than a critical outsider's commentary, or rather than an artist only explaining his or her own intentions in their own work, as is often the case in interviews. The publication would also include excerpts from upcoming books or uncollected pieces of fiction or poetry, or works and illustrations by artists. It was a pantheon of the arts, by and about artists reflecting on each other's creativity.

A few names can be dropped here, to give an idea of the scope of Lou's connections in the world of contemporary North-American letters and beyond, as he only solicited people whose work he valued. The first issue included contributions by Robert Coover, Cid Corman, Toby Olsen, Jerome Rothenberg, Ellen Zweig, and others. Toby Olson became a regular contributor, not just because he was Lou's longstanding friend, but for his invaluable talent and the uncanny fascination his prose narratives exert on his readers.

Number 3, in Spring-Summer 2004, included contributions by Joseph McElroy, Lynn Thompson, Douglas Woolf, and others. The issue was organized in two parts : The Work, and Responses. The Work section was divided into Fiction, Poetry, Commentary, Art Work. And there were three responses to the work of Douglas Woolf, by fellow writers (including Lou, in this case).

The front page advertised the guiding principle sustaining the *Review*, and is worth quoting fully here, as it disappeared from the page later on:

> *Welcome!* Because we cherish life, we cherish the poem as a life-sustaining force. (Robert Kelly, 1965) — *And all work that will nourish you.*
> *We offer, consistently, the most vital contemporary work, and we afford writers and artists space to respond to each other's pieces.*

Quoting a famous contemporary poet (Robert Kelly was born in 1935), this was a statement about where true wealth lay: in the creation of poets as "a life-sustaining force" as well as in the reflection of poets and artists about each other's life-sustaining works. The ambition was great, and the field endless. Lou kept up with this philosophical compass of offering "vital contemporary work" throughout the 23 years of The *Golden Handcuffs Review*, *consistently*, indeed.

Lou began editing The *Golden Handcuffs Review* at the end of 2002 in Seattle, when he was 60 years old, at a turning point in his life because it was also the period when he started devoting his full time to writing. If literature had always been vital to him, in his teaching career as well, his mission of passing on the works he selected to a wider audience was concomitant to the development of his own fiction, in an open, back-and-forth exchange between the production of art and a reflection about its ways and means, its purpose and outreach.

The archives of The *Golden Handcuffs Review*, with the emails for their preparation, may be found at the Archive for New Poetry, in the Special Collections and Archives of the University of California, San Diego, where the Lou Rowan Papers (MSS 806) were deposited in 2018. Such archives are a great source of information for students of the literary and artistic world Lou inhabited, along with his wife, Andrea Augé, whose photography made for some great covers of The *Golden Handcuffs Review*.

I would like to add a personal note on the way Lou worked as an editor. I had the opportunity to collaborate with him on editing an issue of our journal when he was a visiting scholar at Université Sorbonne Paris Nord (formerly Université Paris-XIII). In May 2016, Lou was a guest editor of the special issue of the online journal *Itinéraires : Littérature, Textes, Cultures*. The topic we chose for the 2017-1 issue was *Biography and Fiction*. At the time, Lou was writing a short biography of Linda Farris, and completed his first draft of the chapbook while he was working in France.

Here is an excerpt of how Lou explained his choice for the anglophone writers and scholars he solicited for the issue (while I took care of the francophone contributors):

> Completed the planning and the administrative work for the bilingual biography issue of *Itinéraires* Professor Palleau and I are co-editing.
> [...]
> We contacted the contributors and started to work on the issue. In the process, my contacts from editing *The Golden Handcuffs Review* were very useful.
> [...]
> Contributors to the issue of *Itinéraires* include: [...]
> Miriam Nichols, Professor of literature at Canada's University of Fraser Valley. She will write on her biography-in-progress of the poet Robin Blaser, focusing especially on how to work with the copious documentation this important figure of the '50's-'00's accumulated. She recently published a book of her interviews with Blaser.
> [...]
> I will also contribute an essay on biography for the issue, based on my current work.
> (June 19, 2016, uncollected "Rapport synthétique de séjour à l'Université Paris-XIII")

Needless to emphasize how his humanity and intelligence filter through his comments and praise of the contributors in the report and in his emails. He meant to give an idea of their work, as he was aware that the readers of the administrative report might not know about them. In an additional remark, Lou also wrote, with his usual generosity and kindness: "The editor of a literary journal in the U.S., I found it stimulating to learn about the procedures for editing a serious French journal, and to be the guest editor of one issue." (*ibid.*)

It is of course thanks to him that poet and scholar Rachel Blau DuPlessis, Professor Emerita at Temple University, contributed to the issue with a creative piece which responded beautifully to the theoretical analysis of other excellent scholarly articles in the issue. Lou shared with me the email she sent to him with her piece, in which she wrote :

> Could you do me the enormous favor of reading it and telling me 1) if this is on the right track and 2) if it could go a little longer. The reason I'm asking is—I might have an alternative use for it (i.e. another publication request), where this text might fit. BUT I WANT IT FOR YOU, and this is for many reasons, in part because of the several allusions to French stuff in my life. May I depend on you to tell me soonish. It is attached. warmly, Rachel
> (Uncollected email, July 8, 2016 at 10:54:31 AM PDT, now deposited in the Lou Rowan Papers, quoted with permission from the author)

Rachel Blau DuPlessis did Lou the honor of giving him preference over other publication venues, which says so much about them both, and to this day, I am immensely grateful to them.

The result of this collaboration, a memory I cherish, can be read online : https://journals.openedition.org/itineraires/3651

I feel the need to quote Lou, and one of his correspondents, to convey the trust, the goodwill and friendship he generated around him. To receive an email from him, even after an occasional lapse of contact due to distance, always triggered in me the special feeling of being part of his generous and inclusive circle of kindred spirits. So imagine my surprise when, after many years of hunting for a place in France that would meet Lou and his wife's requirements, one day, on the 29th of November, 2022, Lou sent an email (addressed to my family and me), whose object read : "Hello from Nice!"—bearing the great news of a decisive move to Nice. Lou had celebrated his 80th birthday on the 2nd of January that year and, dauntless in spite of recent health difficulties, had up and left Seattle and his native country :

> After a 2-month siege upon house-selling, long-term French visa obtaining, and finally moving, we are in a small apartment in Nice with the contents of 8 suitcases for the next 3 months while we look for a permanent flat. We are thrilled to be in your country, in no small part because it puts us within reach of you Lizzie and Armance!
>
> We look forward to seeing you down here and up there.
>
> Warmly,
> Andrea and Lou
>
> (private email, Nov. 29, 2022)

From Nice, Lou kept up the good work on The *Golden Handcuffs Review* for the last three years of his life.
What led a Harvard undergraduate, a New York University graduate, a student of theology at Union Theological Seminary in New York, a teacher and a manager at Friends Seminary, an investment banker at Bankers Trust, to become a writer and the editor of an important literary journal in the last 23 years of his career, remains a beautiful mystery to me, but, as one of his fiction titles goes, *A Mystery's No Problem*. (Equus Press, 2016)

Thank you, Lou. Thank you. You were and are much loved.

Collorgues, July 31, 2025

Notes on contributors

Hélène Aji is chair Professor of American literature at the Ecole normale supérieure in Paris, a director of research center UMR 8241 "République des savoirs," and vice-president of the Institut des Amériques. She was Visiting Professor at the University of Texas at Austin in 2017, at the University of Chicago in November 2022, at the Université Libre de Bruxelles in November 2024, and has been a regular Guest Professor at the National and Kapodistrian University of Athens, Greece. She co-edited several journal issues and volumes among which a collection of essays on the poetry of T.S. Eliot (*T.S. Eliot Agoniste*, Éditions Rue d'Ulm, 2024).

Describing the poems in **Rae Armantrout**'s latest book, *Go Figure*, Library Journal says, "she has honed enduring art on the ephemera that constitute a consciousness in motion through the present." Charles Bernstein says, "Her sheer, often hilarious, ingenuity is an aesthetic triumph." Armantrout's 2018 book, *Wobble*, was a finalist for the National Book Award that year. In 2010 Versed won the Pulitzer Prize for Poetry and The National Book Critics Circle Award. Her poems have appeared in many anthologies and journals including Poetry, Conjunctions, Lana Turner, The Nation, The New Yorker, The London Review of Books, Harpers, The Paris Review, Postmodern American Poetry: a Norton Anthology and several editions of The Best American Poetry. She is Professor Emerita at UC San Diego.

Andrea Augé is a photographer, artist, designer, art director (print and film) and an activist for peace and change.

Tony Baker comes from south London, where he spent his youth, and various parts of the north of England, where he spent his early adult life in various employs while writing a thesis on William Carlos Williams. 30 years ago he moved to France for a brief sabbatical and has remained ever since in the Loire valley near Angers where he has worked as an ecologist, translator and primarily a collaborative musician.

Ian Brinton's Most recent publications include *Samuel Beckett (4 Poems)*, a translation of *Quatre Poèmes* (Cornerstone Press, Queensland, 2024), *Language and Death*, a translation of poems by Philippe Jaccottet (Equipage, 2022*), Paul Valéry Selected Poems* (Muscaliet Press, 2021, with a Preface by Michael Heller), *Paris Scenes*, a translation of Baudelaire's '*Tableaux Parisiens*', (Two Rivers Press, 2021). He reviews for PN Review, Litter Magazine, Long Poem Magazine and Golden Handcuffs Review; he co-edits the magazine SNOW and helps curate the Cambridge University Library Archive of Modern Poetry.

Ken Edwards' most recent novel is *Grech* (Grand Iota, 2025). He has published four other novels (*Futures*, *Country Life*, *The Grey Area* and *Secret Orbit*), a memoir of the 1970s (*Wild Metrics*) and sundry other books of prose. His *Collected Poems* was published in 2021 by Shearsman Books. For 25 years he ran the small press Reality Street, and he is now a partner with Brian Marley on Grand Iota. He lives on the south coast of England and plays music with Elaine Edwards as the band Afrit Nebula (with Yair Katz). Both Ken and Elaine remember Lou with great affection.

Louis Grego grew up between Paris and London. A gardening and poetry enthusiast having had Hélène Aji as a university teacher, he has been writing poetry for the past five years. Influenced by contemporary ecopoetics and by social movements of resistance, Louis is currently working to develop a poetry capable of offering a solution to the modern crises by imagining a world of solidarity and care for its living and non-living inhabitants. He is currently undergoing an MPhil in Oxford, focusing his research on contemporary French ecopoetics.

Hank Lazer has published thirty-six books of poetry, including most recently *Abundant Life: New & Selected Poems* (Chax Press), *As We Vanish from Public View* (7 Points Press), and *field recordings of mind in morning* (BlazeVOX, with 15 music-poetry tracks with Holland Hopson on banjo – available on YouTube). In 2025, Lavender Ink published *What Were You Thinking: Essays 2006–2024*. To order books, learn about talks, readings, and workshops, and see photos of Duncan Farm, see Lazer's website: https://www.hanklazer.com. I miss you, Lou!

Stacey Levine is the author of Mice 1961, a finalist for the Pulitzer Prize in fiction. Also the author of *The Girl with Brown Fur*, *Frances Johnson*, and *My Horse and Other Stories*, Levine's fiction has earned a PEN award, and other honors. Her reviews and fiction have appeared in Tin House, Fence, Yeti, The Brooklyn Rail, The Iowa Review, Bookforum, and other venues.

Brian Marley is the author of the novel *Apropos Jimmy Inkling*, the short story collection *The Shenanigans*, and the interlinked photo/fiction book *On Reflection*, all of which are published by Grand Iota.

John Olson is the author of numerous books of poetry and prose poetry, including *Echo Regime*, *Free Stream Velocity*, *Backscatter: New and Selected Poems*, *Larynx Galaxy*, *Dada Budapest*, and *Weave of the Dream King*. Recipient of The Stranger's 2004 Literature Genius Award and 2012 finalist for the Washington State Arts Innovator Award. Novels include *Souls of Wind* (shortlisted for The Believer Book Award, 2008), *The Nothing That Is*, *The Seeing Machine*, *In Advance of the Broken Justy*, and *Mingled Yarn*. *You Know There's Something* (Grand Iota Press, 2023) is his 6th novel. *Unfinished World* (Quale Press, August 2025) will be his 7th.

Françoise Palleau-Papin is Professor of American Literature at the University of Paris XIII-Université Sorbonne Paris Nord, and a member of the multidisciplinary research center PLÉIADE. After completing a PhD dissertation on Willa Cather, she has published a critical monograph on David Markson (*This Is Not a Tragedy*, Dalkey Archive, 2011), and two critical studies, of Willa Cather's novel *My Antonia* (Atlande, 2016) and of Alexis Wright's novel *Carpentaria* (Atlande, 2022). She has edited a critical analysis of William T. Vollmann's novel *The Rifles* (Under Fire, Peter Lang, 2016). With Lou Rowan, she was guest editor of the online special issue of *Itinéraires* 2017/1 on *Biography and Fiction* (http://journals.openedition.org/itineraires/3651). She has translated Patricia Eakins's short stories *The Hungry Girls and Other Stories* (*Les Affamées et autres nouvelles*, UGA Éditions, 2010), and W. S. Merwin's prose narratives "Shepherds" (*Bergers*, Fanlac, 2023) and "Foie Gras" (forthcoming, Fanlac).

Meredith Quartermain is a poetry and prose writer based in Vancouver, Canada. Her most recent books are *Lullabies In the Real World* (2020) and *Things Musing* (2025).

Peter Quartermain's most recent book is *Growing Dumb*, a memoir of boyhood in wartime England. He is the author of two books of critical essays: *Stubborn Poetries and Disjunctive Poetics*, and he edited the *Collected Poems and Plays* of Robert Duncan.

Eléna Rivera is the author of several poetry collections, including *Arrangements* (with Peter Hughes, Aquifer Press), *Epic Series* (Shearsman Books), *Scaffolding* (Princeton University Press), and *The Perforated Map* (Shearsman Books). She received fellowships from the NEA, MacDowell, Trelex Paris Poetry Residency, and the SHOEN Foundation. She lives in New York City.

Aidan Semmens After early poetic activity in 1970s Cambridge, he resumed work on poetry after a 25-year hiatus. Recent collections include *A Stone Dog* (2011), *The Book of Isaac* (2013), *Uncertain Measures* (2014), *Life Has Become More Cheerful* (2017), *There Will Be*

Singing (2020), and *The Jazz Age* (2022). Winner of the 2024 Julia Budenz and Deirdre Roberts prizes. Lives in the northern isles of Scotland.

Jacob Siefring is a literary translator, library professional, and editor of the Empyrean Series for Sublunary Editions. His translations from French include five books by contemporary French author Pierre Senges and a book of poetry by the Belgian writer Émile Verhaeren. He resides in Ottawa, Ontario.

Simon Smith writes poetry, translations, and prose. Latest books: *Municipal Love Poems* (Shearsman Books, 2022), *Last Morning* (Parlor Press, 2022), and *SOURCE with Felicity Allen* (Muscaliet, 2022). Translator of *Catullus* (Carcanet, 2018). Former Poetry Library librarian and university teacher; currently Emeritus Reader in Creative Writing at the University of Kent.

Harriet Tarlo's poetry is published with Shearsman, Etruscan, Guillemot and Wild Pansy Presses and she is the author of numerous essays on poetics, gender, place, walking, collaboration and environment. Her most recent publications are *Cut Flowers* 1 & 2 (2021/2024) and, with Judith Tucker, *Saltwort* (2022). She collaborated for over ten years with the artist Judith Tucker, exhibiting widely here and abroad. She edited the influential anthology *The Ground Aslant: An Anthology of Radical Landscape Poetry* (Shearsman, 2011). She is Professor of Ecopoetry and Poetics at Sheffield Hallam University.

Philip Terry was born in Belfast, poet, translator, and fiction writer. His work includes translations of Perec, Métail, and Queneau. Poetry includes *Oulipoems, Dante's Inferno, and Dictator (a Globish Gilgamesh)*. Editor of *The Penguin Book of Oulipo* (2020) and *The Lascaux Notebooks* (2022). *Purgatorio* (2024) reimagines Dante on Mersea Island.

www.ingramcontent.com/pod-product-compliance
Lightning Source LLC
Chambersburg PA
CBHW042335040426

42446CB00020B/3463